LEVI'S
DREAM

A 1930 trip to the national parks
in a Model A Ford . . . with seven children

LINDA COTTINGTON KILLINGER

MARILEE COTTINGTON McALPINE

KERRY KILLINGER

Prospecta Press

Hardcover ISBN: 978-1-63226-098-7 (privately published)
Paperback ISBN: 978-1-63226-099-4
eBook ISBN: 978-1-63226-126-7

Published by:
Prospecta Press
P.O. Box 3131
Westport CT 06880
(203) 571-0781
Prospectapress.com

Book and cover design by Alexia Garaventa

All proceeds from the sale of this book will be donated to charity via The Kerry and Linda
Killinger Foundation. Visit our website, thekillingerfoundation.org.

1930 road map of the USA used by permission of Rand McNally

Manufactured in the United States of America

This book is dedicated to Grandma and Grandpa
and also to Uncle Jim, Marilee's husband, who passed away
in 2021 while we were writing this book.

Jim and Marilee

Grandma and Grandpa

CONTENTS

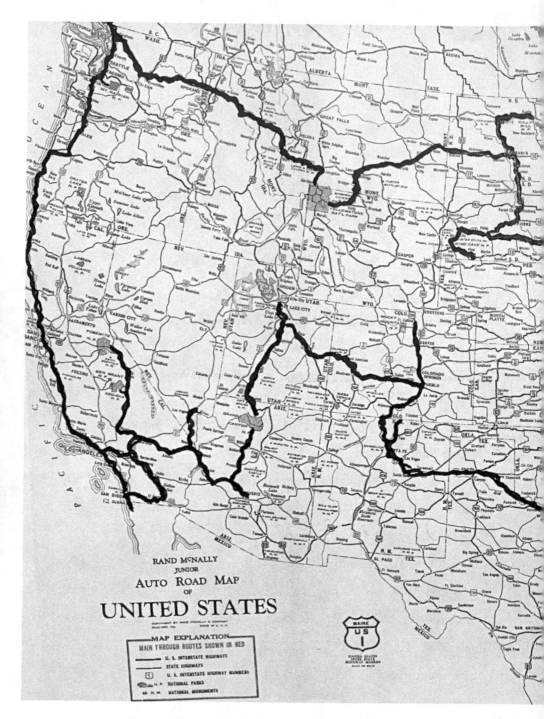

The route of the journey.

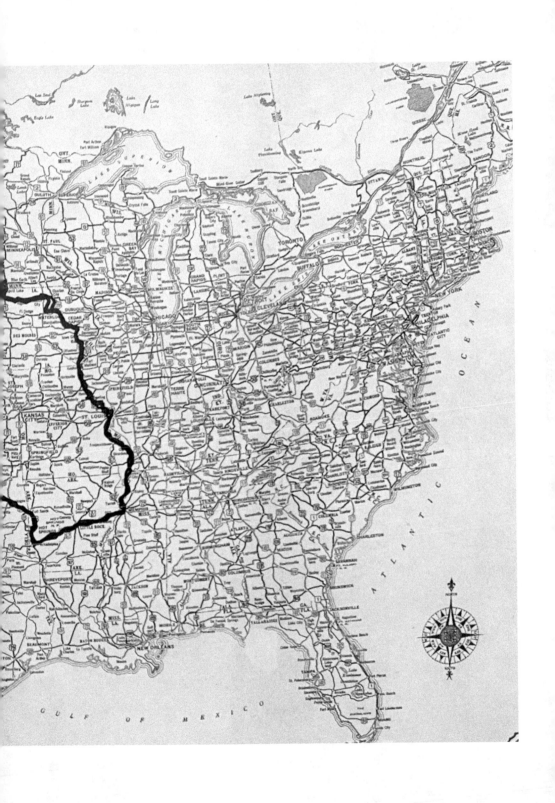

INTRODUCTION

THE ERA BETWEEN WORLD WAR I AND WORLD WAR II WAS ONE OF THE MOST IMPACTFUL TIMES IN OUR COUNTRY'S HISTORY. Thousands of books have been written about this era, which encompassed both World Wars, the 1918 Pandemic, the coming of age of the motor car and the airplane, and the commercialization of our greatest inventions including electricity, indoor plumbing, telephones and the telegraph, and manufacturing mass production. The 40-hour work week and the popularization of vacation time made life a little easier, but the era also held massive labor strikes, and the beginnings of the women's rights movement, which brought women the right to vote in 1920.

The Roaring Twenties brought us the beginnings of mass consumerism, credit, and the dramatic rise of income inequality and wealth concentration in the top 1 percent. The era continued with Prohibition, gangsters, robber barons, our worst farm crisis, the Crash of 1929, the Great Depression, the Dust Bowl, and the loss of half the nation's banks and farms. The structure of our country changed dramatically with the massive exodus from farming to urban manufacturing, the rise of modern management, the good roads movement, and the opening of the national parks to the average American.

So many events that turned the zeitgeist of our country and the world upside down. However, most of the storytelling of that time is narrowly focused on just one or two of these events, centering around a male hero or anti-hero and typically excluding the experiences of women, minorities, and families. Rarely do we see a story about how all these world-shattering events impacted just one ordinary American family.

When we started writing this book, we thought we would write about the simple story of my grandparent's 15-month trip across the country in a 1930 Model A Ford with seven of their thirteen kids, visiting relatives and the national parks.

As we proceeded in the narrative of this book, we realized this was not just a simple story. This was a reveal of how all these historic events in this complex era dramatically affected my family. Not just during the two decades of these events, but in the lasting DNA of future generations. Maybe in the same way these historic events have affected your family.

CHAPTER ONE

1929: LEVI'S DREAM

IT WAS THE SPRING OF 1929 AND MY GRANDPA, LEVI COTTINGTON, HAD A DREAM. It was not the American dream of most people of that era and this was an era of grand dreams. There were those who dreamed of traveling West and claiming their own land. There were those who dreamed of becoming a star in the enticing land of Hollywood. Some were making millions through illegal hauls of alcohol; some were robbing banks. Whatever was forbidden was immediately demanded. The country was filled with citizens who dreamed of riches from gambling in the ever-rising stock market. Stock prices were driven by a frenzy, which seemed to ignore that prices did not begin to reflect the underlying values of the companies. The Wall Street titans were obsessed with their holding companies and investment trusts . . . clever structures meant to lure the public into investments that would mostly allow the titans to skim off the top and leave the investors holding the bag.

Few people in the go-go years of the 1920s ever understood the real ethos robber barons would never confess: the goal of Wall Street was to facilitate speculation and encourage the public to gamble on the margin. A goal they achieved because, by the end of the decade, over half of the stock was purchased "on the margin" with borrowed money. How many ways could they package and repackage investments into instruments with dubious long-term value? After the October 1929 crash, a senior partner of Goldman Sachs confessed to President Roosevelt, "Over speculation and a reckless disregard of economics was the cause of the crash. There was a group [of people] ruthlessly selling short—you could sell anything and depress the market unduly, and the more you depressed it, the more you created panic." A pattern that would repeat itself in the 2008 financial crisis.

My grandpa Levi was not one of those big dreamers. He was a modest and measured man and like many Iowa farmers, rejected the Wall Street schemes for making money. Grandpa's dream was to take time off from the grinding work of managing a 360-acre farm in north central Iowa, in order to spend time with his beloved wife and children on a cross-country trip. He wanted to show his family there was more to life and more to this country than their plot of land in Winnebago County, Iowa, which required them to work from dawn to dusk during one of the most crushing farm depressions in the history of this country. He wanted to inspire his family with a trip to the national parks in the West, visit and connect with relatives scattered around the country, and live for a few months in the intriguing land of southern California. He told his neighbors there were other worlds out there and his children must experience those worlds.

He also was greatly intrigued with the new Ford Model A Standard Fordor. Finally, there was an affordable car that could comfortably hold a large family on a trip across America. The roads were getting safer and easier to travel, and the national parks were finally opened to auto traffic and contained some of the grandest scenery in the world.

However, there was a deeper and more poignant reason for this 15,000-mile trip around the country. It had been a tough decade. The Golden Age of Agriculture that had existed at the turn of the century and expanded during World War I, had crumbled and the 1920s turned out to be one of the toughest decades for farmers. While urban America enjoyed the "Roaring Twenties," speakeasies, the Jazz Age, and a rising and speculative economy, farmers were literally left in the dust. The pricing of farm commodities had plummeted after the war, and farming expenses had risen.

Grandpa was also still recovering from multiple deaths in his family, including the death of his first wife, Etheldra, who died of a stroke in 1913, leaving him a widower with four small children under the age of seven. Just a few months earlier, his seventeen-year-old nephew, Maynard, son of his brother Jacob, died in a drowning accident. Just three years later, his dear mother, Achsa, died from a paralytic stroke and his sister, Elinor, died after that. In 1918, his second wife, my grandma Gertrude Gienap, had a close brush with death. Recently, his beloved father, Levi Sr., a Civil War hero, had also died of a stroke. Trying to manage all this grief and the pressures of supporting eleven children in the middle of a collapsing farm economy, caused Grandpa to be stunned and shattered when he experienced his own stroke. His doctor wisely advised him that he needed to rest and take care of himself.

Faced with the reality of the capricious nature of life, Grandpa wanted to get healthier, relieve stress, and spend time with his wife, my grandma, and their seven youngest children. The four oldest kids would stay and take care of the farm. Grandpa wanted to do everything he could to live a healthier and longer life. He was a gregarious and thoughtful man who was full of adventure and love for his kids. He confided to Grandma often that his sincerest wish was to always have babies in the house. She took the hint and managed to present him with nine children in less than eighteen years (two of the children were born after the trip). My grandparents were not consumed with grabbing more riches or taking part in the go-go, self-absorbed, and frivolous nature of the Roaring Twenties. Instead, my grandparents, like many hard-working Iowa farmers, strode through life knee-deep in decency.

In spite of the tough farming economy, Grandpa was one of the more successful farmers in the community. He had little debt, came from generations of successful farmers, and was an efficient and effective steward of the land. He was well respected in his community and was asked to participate in a number of organizations, including serving as a delegate to the Farm Bureau national convention. He and Grandma rallied all their organizational and business skills and started planning the trip around the country.

Although Grandpa was very excited about the trip, Grandma was a little more circumspect. She loved the idea of the adventure, seeing the remarkable national parks, spending time with her family, escaping the grinding daily chores of a large farm, and visiting relatives. However, she worried the trip could be dangerous for the children, whose ages would range from one to thirteen when they would start the trip. She had read there were grizzly bears, buffaloes, wolves and other dangerous creatures in the national parks. How does one protect your children in that environment? She felt safe camping near relatives, but were the public camps really safe? Over the last decade, thousands of people crossed the country in their motor cars, but she hadn't heard of any other couple taking their seven young children with them.

They knew it would take about a year to plan for the trip. The most important task for the next year would be to prepare their twenty-one-year-old son, Lyle, and his wife Gayle, to take over the farm for nearly two years, while they traveled. Lyle and Gayle were married in 1929 and eventually would have four children. Lyle would receive help from his younger brothers, Don, age nineteen and Dwight, age seventeen, but this was a lot of responsibility for people their age. The oldest daughter, Gladys, had married Ole Siekmeier in 1927. They had their own farm just a few miles from Forest City, and eventually had six children.

My grandparents also knew the trip needed to start right after school was out in May 1930. That would give them three months to take the northern route of their trip, through Yellowstone National Park, and allow them time to find a home in Los Angeles to rent for nine months so the older kids could enroll in California schools. Their southern route back would start in June 1931, traveling through the Grand Canyon and other national parks, getting back to Iowa in late August 1931. Just in time for the kids to go back to school in Forest City.

They started their preparations by ordering maps of the United States and sent for a number of travel guides that identified good roads, camp sites, and mileage between towns. They read national magazines about the new motor car traveling mania in the country, studied the Sears catalog for camping equipment, and asked for advice from Iowa neighbors who had traveled to California by train or motor car. They contacted close relatives who lived around the country and included them in their route. The schedule would definitely include a week-long stay with Grandpa's cousin, Lee Spaulding, in Wenatchee, Washington. The two cousins were life-long friends and had invested together in an apple orchard in Wenatchee. Each year, Cousin Lee would load up railroad cars with the apples he had grown and send them to Grandpa, who sold them to Iowans, who loved the crisp, delicious Washington apples.

My grandparents carefully planned the routes and developed a detailed trip schedule and calculated a tight budget for the trip. They calculated the trip to California and back, plus sight-seeing while living in California for nine months, would total at least 15,000 miles of driving. The Model A gas tank held 11 gallons of gas and they could average about 14 miles per gallon, so they could drive about 154 miles on a tank of gas. Gas was up to 50 cents in the rural areas, but only 9 cents a gallon in Los Angeles, averaging around 20 cents a gallon. If they drove 15,000 miles, they would need about 97 tanks of gas averaging $2.20 a tank for a total of $214 for gas. Some of the road guides indicated they could drive about 300 miles a day if there were good roads. However, many of the roads were rough so it was common to routinely blow out tires and require other repairs. They budgeted about $200 for oil, spark plugs, tires, repairs, and any other surprises.

Camping with relatives would be free, but public camps could cost up to $2 a night. They figured they would stay in public camps about half the time, so they budgeted about $100 for camping. Food and entertainment would run a modest $20 a week for nine people, because they would cook all their meals and would rarely eat in restaurants. For the 15-month trip, those costs would be about $1200. Rent for a house in California would be about $20 a month, so rent would add up to $180 for the nine-month period. If extra money was needed, it could be telegraphed to them through Western Union.

These budgeted costs added up to about $1894, so Grandpa purchased $2,000 worth of American Express traveler's checks for the trip. In 1930, American Express advertised:

> The cheques were perfectly safe, worry-proof travel funds. Millions of travelers in the past 39 years carried $2 billion in American Express traveler's checks. The new small blue cheques fit cozily into a woman's handbag like a compact, or into a man's pocket like a cardcase. The cheques come in denominations of $10, $20, $50, and $100. They can be purchased for 75 cents for each $100 at 22,000 banks across the country.

The most important purchase for the trip was finding the perfect family motor car. It would have to be roomy enough to accommodate nine people, and sturdy enough to carry a camping tent, camp beds, clothes, utensils, and tools. The next step was searching for a tent that would attach to the car so they could camp out at relatives' homes as well as the ubiquitous auto camps found in nearly every town and national park around the country.

At night, after the kids were in bed, my grandparents poured over the latest Sears Roebuck Catalog for their camping gear. Their first big find was on page 501 of the 1100-page catalog—a "Cross country waterproof tourist or automobile tent" for only $18.85. This popular tent was shed-shaped, with two large marquisette screened windows and a cover flap that would attach to the car. They decided they would need three "camp beds." The metal beds cost $7.98, had short legs, springs, and were "double" size, light weight, and advertised as "easily set up or taken down and occupying such a small space when folded, that it is very convenient as a camp bed or a spare bed in any home." Each Kapok cot mattress for the beds was covered with heavy khaki denim, measured 48-by-76 inches, and cost $4.48.

The Sears catalog at the time served as a metaphor for the Roaring Twenties and the ramped-up stock market. The economy and consumerism expanded exponentially in the 1920s, mostly fed by the rise of the acceptability and availability of credit. People could buy nearly anything on credit, including anything in the Sears catalog. Sears bragged in their 1928 catalog that one could buy anything on credit and "no interest or other expenses would be added to the monthly payment prices." Reading this, the average consumer would expect no interest would be added—one could get credit for "free." However, it was a ruse. For example, a small radio in the Sears catalog sold for $54.95 cash or it could be bought on credit with a down payment of $9, five monthly payments of $9, plus a last payment of $5.95 for a total cost of "only" $59.95. This meant there was interest—$5.00 over a period of six months, which calculates to an annual interest rate of about 20 percent. By the end of the 1920s, credit was used to purchase 90 percent of all consumer goods. These fantasy economics of debt accumulation have suckled every economic downturn since 1929. Fortunately, my grandparents were not swayed by the clarion call of debt and believed in all-cash payments.

Grandma spent the next year sewing clothes for all the children on the trip. She had to calculate how much the kids would grow in the next two years, who could wear hand-me-downs, and who would need new clothes. She set about sewing fourteen new dresses for Marilee, who was born on March 23, 1929, a year before the trip. She also sewed coats for the kids and calculated what shoes would be needed.

It was tricky figuring out the sleeping arrangements. The four oldest kids, Keith, Pauline, Richard, and Gwen would sleep in two camp beds in the tent. Grandma and Grandpa would sleep on a camp bed between the tent and the car. The three youngest would sleep in the car with one-year-old Marilee sleeping in the front seat. When they were driving, the four oldest would sit in the back seat and the three youngest would sit in the front seat, with Marilee sitting on grandma's lap. Can you imagine driving 15,000 miles cross-country with seven kids and no car seats, seat belts, strollers, pack-and-plays, iPads, iPhones, or gaming machines? How can you possibly make a cross-country trip without video screens embedded in the back of the front seats?

My grandparents also purchased a Sears 18-quart "Kook Kwick" steam pressure cooker for $18.75. It was described as having a "simplified locking device, with one simple, quick tightening screw." The catalog assured the customer the pressure cooker contained "No danger of scorching or burning." The device had three pie-shaped pans that one could layer inside the cooker and the Sear's ad promised the "device was built to last a lifetime and supply the family with nutritious food." The family planned that every day they would buy meat, potatoes and vegetables at local grocery stores and farm stands along the way, and pressure cook them for dinner on the gas cook stove. The meat would go in the bottom layer, next would go potatoes, and vegetables were steamed in the top layer.

Grandpa made a deal with Grandma: if she would make the meals, he would keep the seven children occupied. Grandma enthusiastically accepted the deal.

While they planned their route, they were looking at motor cars for the trip. The 1930 Ford Model A Standard Fordor looked like the perfect car for them. The car contained two large bench seats for the family, windshield wipers, safety glass, and a hard top with real roll-up windows. There was a factory-built trunk on the back and a built-in toolbox attached to the front fender—all for less than $800. The first commercially successful motor car radio was available in 1930 and cost $130, but I doubt Grandpa would have sprung for a radio.

A few years before, Grandpa had purchased a Model T from the local Forest City Ford dealer and found it to be a reliable and useful car. However, the Model T was too small, open air, slow, and unsafe for an extensive trip with seven kids. There were three major improvements that made this trip possible in 1930: The good roads movement, the new Model A Ford, and access to the national parks.

THE GOOD ROADS MOVEMENT

There never was a need before the arrival of the motor car, to have "good roads" leading into the western half of the country. When Lewis and Clark made their breathtaking exploration of the Louisiana Purchase from 1804–1806, the majority of the future western states like California, Nevada, Texas, Arizona, Utah, and New Mexico, were part of the Spanish Territory. When gold was discovered in Sutter's Mill, California in January of 1848, everything changed. Suddenly there was a need to find a way to get to California. Days after the discovery of gold, the Treaty of Guadalupe Hidalgo was signed, ending the Mexican–American War. The treaty gave the US the Rio Grande River as a boundary for Texas, plus the ownership of California, Nevada, Utah, Colorado, half of New Mexico, and most of Arizona. Texas became a state in 1845, California in 1850, Nevada in 1864, Colorado in 1876, Utah in 1896, and Arizona and New Mexico in 1912. Now this was all our country and people were itching to explore it. Between 1848 and the 1870s, hundreds of thousands of gold-seekers and settlers invaded California by land and sea, in search of their fortune. Some made the arduous journey on ships from Oregon, Hawaii, Mexico, South America, and China. Some sailed from the east coast of the US to the east coast of Panama, hiked across the country to the Pacific Ocean, and took a ship to California. Others sailed the long, precarious route around Cape Horn, the southernmost point of South America.

Other adventurers took the land route either in small groups, stagecoaches, or wagon trains that followed several trails, with most starting from Independence, Missouri. The most famous of these trails was the Oregon Trail, which had a span of over 2,000 miles. Other paths included the Santa Fe Trail, the Chisholm Trail, the California Trail, the Mormon Trail, and the Old Spanish Trail. From 1836 to 1869 more than 420,000 pioneers took the four-to-six-month journey west on wagon trains, with over 40,000 dying along the way.

During the Civil War, Congress, after heavy lobbying from the railroads, decided the best way to "settle the West" was to extend the railroad system past the Missouri River. In 1863, the Pacific Railroad Act chartered the Central Pacific and the Union Pacific Railroad companies, with building a transcontinental railroad that would link the east to the west. One railroad started in Sacramento and the other in Council Bluffs, Iowa. Over the next six years, the two companies competed in a heated race and finally met at Promontory, Utah on May 10, 1869, as dramatically outlined in the Stephen Ambrose book, *Nothing Like it in The World*. The months-long wagon train trips were no longer necessary—the railroad could get people to California in just a few days, with hardly any casualties.

Prior to the completion of the transcontinental railroad in 1869, there were only 45,000 miles of railway tracks in the US, mostly in the eastern part of the country; however, within thirty years, another 170,000 miles were added. The railroads enjoyed the benefits of having decades of monopoly transportation across the country, up until the 1920s when the motor car stole the show. Four of the five transcontinental railroads were built with federal land grants, which came with millions of acres of free public land. In order to attract settlers and tourists, the railroads sold some of the land to finance the construction of the railways as well as the construction of the towns, hotels, and other facilities along the way.

However, by the first decade of the twentieth century, the railroads had become the industrial "establishment"—arrogant, impersonal, bureaucratic, and monopolistic. The trains routinely transported almost half a billion passengers a year, whistling through the country at 40 to

60 mph. As the crowds grew, the schedules constantly changed, the wait times were unpredictable, service was terrible, and people longed for the freedom to travel on their own. *The American Motorist* journal of the Automobile Association, declared that the railways had, "robbed the roads of that picturesque and free means of travel [the stagecoach] and nothing ever took its place until the dawn of the motor car." By around 1920, the number of train tracks had exploded to 254,000 miles, but that paled next to the three million miles of roads (two-thirds of them rural) available for the motor car, and the public demanded these old rural roads become drivable.

Unfortunately, most of those roads in the West were rough, muddy paths that made it very difficult to travel very far in a motor car. Many states had constitutional prohibitions against funding road projects, and federal highway programs were not funded until the late 1920s. Although many of the urban roads were paved, only 9 percent of the two million miles of rural roads had improved surfaces like gravel, stone, sand-clay, brick, or oiled earth. It is not surprising the public was starting to demand better roads to accommodate their new passion— traveling the country in their motor cars!

The first known person to accomplish a transcontinental trip in a motor car across these miserable roads was H. Nelson Jackson in 1903. This was also the year the Wright brothers made the first sustained flight by a manned heavier-than-air-powered aircraft. The first woman to make the cross-country motor car trip from New York to San Francisco, was Alice Ramsey in 1909. Her book about the adventure, *Veil, Duster, and Tire Iron,* detailed the trip across the country with her three girlfriends.

Alice wanted to prove that a perfectly normal young mother was capable of driving a car across the country without help from a man. When the Maxwell-Briscoe Automobile Company (which later became the Chrysler Corporation) heard of her desire, they knew they had found their perfect public relations ploy. Motor car companies had figured out women were the "new" untapped customers. Maxwell supplied Alice with a dark green, four-cylinder, 30-horsepower 1909 Maxwell DA. It had two bench seats, a removable roof, and open windows. The auto company helped her develop the route across the country, and then informed all the newspapers about her travels. Maxwell also arranged for local guides and a group of pilot cars to follow her, just in case she ran into trouble. However, Alice insisted on changing the tires and performing maintenance and repairs on the car. The promotion worked. The women were greeted with enthusiasm by dignitaries in every town, stayed in the best hotels, and ate in the best restaurants. They were a hit! Nearly fifty years later, the Automobile Manufacturers Association claimed that Alice's trip "helped mightily to convince the skeptics that automobiles were here to stay—rugged and dependable enough to command any man's respect, gentle enough for the daintiest lady."

Because most motor cars were open-air and the roads were dusty and muddy, Alice and her friends wore goggles, and long rubber ponchos, with sleeves shirred at the wrist bound into elastic hems. Their hats were also rubber and anchored down with a long scarf. Alice relied on directions from the *1909 Automotive Blue Book Guide*, but since there were no highway numbers or any signage along the way, a typical instruction read: "After 11.6 miles, there is a yellow house and a bar on the right—turn left." Heaven help you if the house had been torn down or painted another color. Alice's trip took 59 days, covered 3,800 miles, and ended in California with the *San Francisco Chronicle* declaring, "Pretty Women Motorists Arrive After Trip Across the Continent."

In spite of the insufferable roads, Alice had inspired suffragists to become one of the first groups of women to utilize and drive the motor car on their own, "barnstorming" across the country promoting the women's right to vote.

With all this barnstorming going on, the motor car industry was growing fast with hundreds of manufacturers supplying parts, tires, and camping gear for the eager new band of "tourists" and "sightseers." However, in order for their industries to thrive and prosper, they

Alice Ramsey changing a tire. Courtesy of the Detroit Public Library

needed a reliable highway across the nation. So, in 1912, a number of industry leaders developed the Lincoln Highway Association, with the goal of developing the first transcontinental highway. The thirteen officers included the presidents of Packard Motor Car, Hudson Motor Car, Detroit National Bank, Goodyear Tire and Rubber, Portland Cement, American State Bank in Detroit, Ohio auto manufacturer Willys-Overland, and Carl Fisher, founder of the Indianapolis Motor Speedway and the Prest-O-Lite auto parts company. Henry Ford would not join their group, because he knew private ownership of roads involved expensive tolls and he believed the government should pay for roads and make them free to everyone.

The goal of the Lincoln Association was to privately raise money and finish the cross-country highway before the 1915 Panama-Pacific International Expositions in San Francisco and San Diego. The Expos were created to recognize the rebuilding of San Francisco after the 1906 earthquake, as well as celebrate the completion of the Panama Canal.

In order to raise money for the "construction" of the highway, the group initiated what was probably one of the first crowdsourcing, fund-raising events in this country. The ads for the Lincoln Highway declared that for $1,000 or more, one could become a "Founder of the Highway," and for as little as $5, one could become a "member."

The Lincoln Highway Association didn't actually build a new road across the country, but rather cobbled together 3,400 miles of roads that ran through 13 states, starting at Times Square in New York City, rolling across Iowa, and ending in Lincoln Park in San Francisco. The system was dedicated in 1913. Most of the roads were primitive, often nothing more than sand or packed earth. By 1920, an estimated 20,000 drivers had driven the entire route, which typically took two to three weeks. By the end of the 1930s, all but 42 miles of the Highway were surfaced.

In 1915, before she was an etiquette guru, Emily Post drove the twenty-seven-day trip across the country on the new Lincoln Highway, so she could attend the Pan-Pacific Expositions in San Francisco and San Diego. She also was sponsored by the Maxwell auto company, held interviews at every stop, and wrote articles about her trip for *Collier's*, a popular weekly magazine. She carefully chronicled the trip in her book, *By Motor to the Golden Gate*, which became one of the first personalized auto travel guides for those who preferred the best hotels and restaurants along the way. Her goal was to encourage upper-class women to drive the route, even though the men folk would probably disapprove. Astutely attuned to luxury, she described her hotel in Chicago: "For $3.50 a night you can get a small, light, and comfortable room, for $7 you can have a room overlooking the lake. Both included bathrooms and all the latest Ritz-Carlton type of furnishings." She recommended her readers would need a "heavy coat, sweater, duster, and hat," as well as formal clothes for hotel dining, velvet slippers for evening, and cold cream to prevent sunburn. Her biggest complaint, like most travelers in that era, was saved for the gumbo roads across Iowa, which fostered a "vicious and viscous impassable brand of mud peculiar to the state." Others complained the Iowa mud roads were "a predatory vampire, insatiable, long-armed, and wicked to a bottomless depth."

The roads across Iowa were so contentious that the campaign for Iowa governor in 1916 was fought over the "mud roads" candidate vs. the "paved roads" candidate. At that time, 15 percent of the Iowa population had motor cars, but only 400 of the 100,000 miles of Iowa roads had any kind of permanent surfacing. The mud roads (no more taxes) candidate won and the Iowa legislature celebrated by attempting to abolish the State Highway Department.

However, the need for a cross-country road system wasn't just for locals and tourists. In 1919, the automakers, gasoline companies, and tire manufacturers prodded the War Department to organize a cross-country caravan of army vehicles. The purpose of the trip was not only to take a WWI victory lap, but also to test the capabilities of the vehicles and highlight the poor state of America's roads. A side mission of this trip was to discover what it would take to create a road system that would allow the army to mobilize quickly for national security.

Meanwhile in the Washington, D.C area, a 28-year-old lieutenant colonel named Dwight D. Eisenhower, was cooling his heels stateside training recruits for battle, when he really wanted to be fighting in France. He worried that with the war over, the army would downsize and his military career could be over. So when he heard about the army trip, he eagerly signed up for what he thought would be a great adventure driving across the muddy, teeth-chattering, unpaved roads of America. On July 7, 1919, the 81-vehicle army convoy of tanker trucks, field kitchens, ambulances, 250 enlisted men, 24 officers, and numerous passenger cars carrying reporters, took off from Washington, D.C. The caravan traversed 3,242 miles through eleven states in 62 days, averaging 52 miles a day. Probably creeping along the road at an average of about 5 miles per hour. This speaks to the state of the roads and the condition of the army vehicles at the time.

Eisenhower later concluded that, "It seemed evident that a very small amount of money spent at the proper time would have kept the roads in good condition." When Eisenhower became the Supreme Commander of the Allied Forces in World War II, he saw first-hand how Nazi Germany's high-speed autobahn allowed its troops to mobilize quickly to fight on two fronts. Eisenhower reasoned that, "After seeing the autobahns of modern Germany, I decided as president, to put an emphasis on this kind of road building." This was the inspiration

Eisenhower with WWI army tank. Courtesy of the Eisenhower Library

for the creation of the Interstate Highway System, appropriately named the "Dwight D. Eisenhower National System of Interstate and Defense Highways."

Around the same time the Lincoln Highway Association was planning its route across the country, the officers of the Association of State Highway Officials (AASHO) decided that the dozens of named highways were too confusing and believed a numbering system for highways would be an easier navigating tool for drivers. Not only was there a Lincoln Highway, but there were a number of "named highways" all over the country including the Old Spanish Trail from St. Augustine to San Diego; the National Old Trails Highway from Baltimore to LA going through Santa Fe; the Pike's Peak Ocean to Ocean Highway from New York to LA; the Theodore Roosevelt International Highway from Portland, Maine to Portland, Oregon; and many others.

In 1914, the AASHO officers began a decade-long lively debate about how to number the new highways in their states. For some reason, many officers were hoping that Route 66 would go through their states. The stakes were astronomical. Finally, after a decade of debate, the numbering system was complete. Odd numbers were given to highways running north and south and even numbers for east to west. The head of these daring highway officials was Cy Avery from Tulsa,

Oklahoma, who had already ordered 600,000 maps claiming Route 66 would go through his hometown of Tulsa. He fought tooth and nail for this honorific and finally won! The book, *Father of Route 66*, describes his promotional efforts that turned the route into an American Icon.

By 1930, when my family took their trip, there were 23 million registered passenger cars in this country, thousands of people were exploring the West, and nearly 90 percent of the roads had some type of surface. The roads in a few areas were still an adventure, but the sights and sounds were the most provocative in the world.

CHAPTER TWO

1909—1920: THE GOLDEN AGE OF AGRICULTURE AND THE EMERGING AGE OF AUTO AND AIR TRANSPORTATION

THE GOLDEN AGE OF AGRICULTURE IN IOWA BY 1909 WAS SO PROSPEROUS THAT WHEN MY GRAND-MA GERTRUDE GIENAP WAS ONLY THIRTEEN YEARS OLD, HER FAMILY COULD AFFORD TO BOOK A "CRUISE" TO GERMANY AND SPEND FOUR MONTHS VISITING FAMILY. Both her father and mother—Herman and Martha—were born in Germany: Herman in Wittenburg, and Martha in Rugen. Rugen is Germany's largest island and lies in the Baltic Sea north of Germany and south of Sweden. The 358-square-mile island is a very popular tourist destination because of its long, sandy beaches, lagoons, and open bays. The chalky-colored cliffs of the Jasmund peninsula stand over 500 feet in the air, embedded with deep green forests surrounded by the bright blue sky and the deep blue Baltic Sea. This is about as dramatically different from Iowa as you can get. However, for all its beauty, Rugen was somewhat of a foster child passed back and forth through the centuries among Sweden, Germany, the Holy Roman Empire, Prussia, and France.

On June 17, 1909, *The Webster City [Iowa] Journal* proudly announced the "Herman Gienap family left on Monday for Germany." Actually, truth be told, my grandma, her mom, Martha, her fifteen-year-old brother, Walter, and her two sisters, seven-year-old Alice and two-year-old Esther, left for Germany in June and Herman stayed in Webster City to tend the farm. He joined them in late August.

Not too much is known about my great-grandpa Herman Gienap or his life in Germany. He was a very skilled craftsman who worked in a shop in Berlin that made carriages for the Kaiser Wilhelm. He came to the US in 1889 when he was twenty-two years old. Since he had very little money, he earned his passage as a ballast worker—a tough way to travel. In the nineteenth century, sometimes a ship would use ballast like bricks, sand, slate, coal, and flagstone to distribute weight and keep the ship upright and balanced. When Herman settled in Iowa, he became a successful farmer, although he often stated that he preferred carpentry to farming.

Martha Lestmann Gienap's father owned a shoe store in Rugen but died when Martha was only two-years-old. Three years later her mother, a practical nurse, died from pneumonia in her early thirties. Martha's grandmother took over the care of Martha and her older sister Mary, but the grandmother died just a few months later. Much like the island of Rugen itself, Martha and Mary were tossed about like foster children among the remaining relatives. Finally an aunt and uncle from Webster City, adopted the two girls and brought them to Iowa. Martha spoke English, but she never learned to read English and continued to read the German newspaper that was printed in Stanhope, Iowa.

The first investigation I wanted to pursue about the trip to Germany was tracking down the steamship taken by my grandma's family. After days of unfruitful research reading lists of names on dozens of ship manifests, I called my sister to commiserate. I told her I was shocked at how many ships there were galloping across the ocean in 1909 between Europe and the United States. Hundreds! Hundreds! My sister quietly listened to my rants and then revealed, "No problem. Forty years ago Grandma gave me dozens of postcards from that trip. Let me look, I think there are post cards of the ships." For the first time in my extremely verbal life, I was stunned into complete silence. My sister was grateful for the rare moment.

The ship my great-grandma Martha Gienap and the four kids took to Germany was the *Cincinnati* from the Hamburg-Amerika Linie. The ship had four masts, two steam funnels and cruised along at 16 knots. It held accommodations for 243 guests in first class, 210 in second, 484 in third and 1,821 in fourth. To give perspective, three years after the *Cincinnati* first sailed, the famous *Titanic* sank on its 1912 maiden voyage. The "biggest ship of its time," the *Titanic* held 2,435 passengers and was 882 feet long. Grandma's ship held 2,758 passengers but was only 582 feet long. The *Titanic* was 50 percent longer with 15 percent fewer passengers! However, interior pictures of the *Cincinnati* revealed a ship that appeared almost as elegant. It had a large carved staircase, a domed sunroof with stained glass windows, and a velvet draped ballroom. The *Cincinnati* also had a short life. In 1917, it was seized by the US during WWI and in 1918 the ship was torpedoed and sunk near the French coast by a U-86 German submarine.

The *Cincinnati's* maiden voyage was on May 27, 1909, from Hamburg, Germany. The ship stopped in Southampton, England, Cherbourg, France, and finally arrived in New York City just a few days later. Grandma's family took a train from Webster City, Iowa, to New York City and boarded the ship in early June. Once Grandma arrived in

Germany, she quickly bought a ship postcard to mail to her father and wrote, "Dear Papa, I have written a letter so I won't write much here. This is the picture of the steam ship. Love, Gertrude." The postcard was sent to Webster City, R.F.D. 6, Iowa, U.S.A. No addresses or zip codes existed at the time. After reading a number of letters from Grandma to her papa, she appeared to adore her father, just like most thirteen-year-old girls.

Great-grandpa Herman had a much faster trip to Germany in late August. His ship, the *Deutschland*, had four steam funnels, two masts, and sped along at 23 knots, crossing the Atlantic Ocean in only five days. The ship had 467 guests in first class, 300 in second and 300 in steerage for a total of 1,067 passengers. On the return trip in October, the entire family took the *President Grant* ship from the Hamburg-Amerika Linie. She was about 600 feet long and had six masts, but only one steam funnel, so she was much slower, with an average speed of only 14 knots. There were about 1,800 passengers and the price of the one-way ticket was 18 pounds for first class, and 10 pounds for second class. During their trip back, the seas were violent and nearly everyone on board was sick and remained in their cabins. Normally, the second-class passengers were not allowed in first class, but with everyone sick, Grandma and her brother, Walter, had the run of the ship. The *President Grant* had a much longer life than the other ships. She also was seized by the US in 1917, served in WWI, but survived long enough to carry troops to the Pacific in WWII.

During the trip to Germany, Grandma's postcards revealed they had extensive travels throughout the country, including the beautiful island of Rugen, the bustling metropolis of Hamburg, with its heavy gothic architecture, and Great-Grandpa's hometown of Wittenburg with its simple brick homes with high steep roofs. Grandma had also collected several postcards of Wilhelm II, the German Emperor and King of Prussia and his first wife, Princess Augusta Victoria of Schleswig-Holstein-Sonderburg-Augustenburg. Wilhelm reigned from June 1888 until November 1918.

1909 postcards of the interior and exterior of the President Grant ship

During the fall of 1909, Grandma and her family traveled to Berlin to watch a large military parade and saw Emperor Wilhelm II and his princess at the height of their glory. Grandma and her family checked out the parade to see if they could find any carriages that Herman may have helped build for the emperor. Nearly a decade after this proud military parade, the emperor's tactless public statements and erratic foreign policy moves antagonized the international community. He was considered by many to be one of the underlying causes of WWI. When the German war effort collapsed after a series of crushing defeats on the Western Front in 1918, Wilhelm was forced to abdicate, bringing an end to the nearly 1000-year monarchy reign of the House of Hohenzollern.

When the Gienap family returned to Iowa in October 1909, the Golden Age of Agriculture continued to bless Iowa farmers. Commodity prices for farm crops were historically high, averaging 32 percent higher than prices at the turn of the century, and costs remained low. The explosion of immigration in the US, as well as the European demands for our crops during WWI increased the demand for food. The relative purchasing power of farmers' income during this period was higher than any other time in American history.

In the later years of the Golden Age of Agriculture, my grandma Gertrude Gienap and my grandpa Levi Cottington lived completely different lives and didn't know each other, even though they were both born and raised on farms near Webster City. Grandpa was born on February 29, 1884, and Grandma was born eleven years later on November 7, 1895. Grandpa and his first wife, Etheldra Sarah Parry, were married in 1902 when Grandpa was only eighteen years old and she was nearly twenty. However, Grandpa liked to joke that since he was a leap year baby, he was only four years old when he married. They farmed one of Levi Sr.'s farms in the Tunnel Mill area on the Boone River, seven miles south of Webster City. Their first child, Gladys, was born in 1905, followed by Lyle in 1907, Donald in 1910, and Dwight in 1912.

Just a few months after the birth of Dwight, Etheldra was taken ill and died of a stroke on April 14, 1913. The *Webster City Daily Freeman* reported that she "was a young woman about thirty and well known in her own community and to many in this city. Her sad taking away will be mourned by all who are acquainted with the family."

Grandpa became a widower with four small children ages seven, five, two, and six-month-old Dwight. Fortunately, Grandpa was surrounded by the large and supportive Cottington family, which included his six brothers and sisters and dozens of cousins, who all chipped in to help the widowed father.

My grandpa Levi's family was headed by my great-grandpa, Levi Sr., who came over to America in 1841 as a small baby in a tiny sailboat, piloted by his father, Jesse. They first settled in Waterville, New York, where my great-great-grandpa, Jesse, worked on the Palmer Hop farm for several years. Hops are green cone-shaped flowers which contain the yellow pods that provide the bitterness, aroma, and flavor in beer. In 1851, Jesse bought a farm in Wisconsin, where he was credited with bringing hops to that state. When the Civil War broke out, my great-grandpa, Levi Sr., immediately enlisted in Company F of the 3rd Wisconsin Calvary. He was stationed in Ft. Scott, Kansas, where he cast his first vote for Abraham Lincoln. Most of his war experiences consisted of riding his horse scouting for "bushwhackers," the southern rebels who were sniping at union soldiers.

In 1867, Levi Sr. was either taken ill or severely wounded by the bushwhackers and sent back to a hospital in Wisconsin, where he fell in love with and married his nurse, Achsa. They decided to move to Iowa and grab some of the land warrants available to Civil War veterans. Union veterans of the Civil War received special homestead rights in 1870, when amendments to the 1862 Homestead Act gave them the right to claim 160 acres within railroad grant areas and deduct the length of their war service from the five-year residency needed to qualify for a homestead. Military warrants accounted for nearly 40 percent of all Iowa land acquisitions. Seventy thousand Iowans fought for the

Union and 21,053 were either killed or seriously wounded. Thousands came back to Iowa, applied for the grants, and became farmers.

In 1867, Levi Sr. and his bride Achsa acquired farmland near Webster City and navigated a prosperous tide of farming in the late 1800s and early 1900s. He became a community leader and held various township and school board offices, was elected to several terms on the county board of supervisors and the city council of Webster City, served on the Soldiers Relief Commission, ran for the state legislature as a Teddy Roosevelt progressive, and was hailed as a brave Civil War hero.

The *Webster City Freeman Tribune* described him as:

> . . . a man noted for honor and integrity and possesses the full confidence and respect of his fellow men. No one owes a greater debt of appreciation or held a warmer or more lasting place in the general esteem. He was one of this country's most useful and respected pioneers. The men who made this part of the country what it is were of heroic quality. He was brought to this country when he was only a baby, but so absorbed the spirit and ideals of his adopted country that no native-born citizen surpassed him in either the quality of his patriotism or in devotion to duty and the ideals of what citizenship requires of true manhood.

My great-grandpa, Levi Sr., was described as short, with a distinguished white beard, a lyrical voice, and a jolly attitude. His wife, Achsa, was taller and always wore a white cloth cap, an old English custom. My great-aunt Faith described her father, Levi Sr., as "fine, loving, understanding, and the greatest influence in my life. Even now when I have problems, I feel his presence and remember his words of courage, which helps me carry on." Levi Sr. and Achsa would eventually have seven children, including my grandpa, Levi, Jr.

Great-grandpa Levi Sr with his favorite plow horses—June and Daisy

After the death of Grandpa Levi's first wife, Etheldra, he struggled as a grieving widower, while at the same time, my grandma Gertrude was graduating the eighth grade from the one-room schoolhouse near her farm. In those days, it was not uncommon for kids to go right to college from the eighth grade. My great-grandpa Herman Gienap was determined to have all three of his daughters go to college so they could support themselves if something happened to their husbands. Ironically, neither one of Grandma's sisters got married and both had long careers as teachers. Education has always been important to Iowans, so there were many options. Grandma could have attended the Iowa Teacher's College, Iowa State University, or even the University of Iowa. There were also dozens of private colleges around the state, typically affiliated with churches.

However, Grandma was intrigued with the idea of going to school in the big city—Des Moines. Many of the private schools in the state would not allow women, but there was a small college in Des Moines, named Highland Park, that accepted women. The college was first opened by a syndicate of real estate holders in the Highland Park suburb, who thought a college would enhance the value of their real estate. They wanted the college to offer both men and women "a practical

Grandma's (on the left) college dorm room

education, by providing small classes that emphasized reading, discussion, and the application of knowledge."

In the fall of 1911, when Grandma was fifteen, she enrolled as a business major at the Highland Park Normal College. At the time, the college had several standard majors: engineering, liberal arts, music, oratory, pedagogy (the practice of teaching), business, and pharmacy. Pretty hefty subjects for a small college. Grandma graduated with a business degree on July 31, 1913, at the age of seventeen. It is unclear what Grandma did after graduation, but at the end of December 1914, the *Jewell Record* in Hamilton County reported that, "Gertrude and [her older brother] Walter left town to spend the winter with relatives in Guthrie, Oklahoma." Despite the long distances, my great-grandma Martha Gienap and her children were very close to Martha's sister, Mary. As adopted orphans from Germany, Martha and Mary had been through a lot together and always stayed in touch.

Grandma probably returned from Oklahoma in the spring of 1915, but it is unclear when she met Grandpa and how long they dated. However, in late October 1916, Grandma had a secret. She was twenty years old, unmarried, and expecting a baby. She knew her strict, German Lutheran parents would not take it well. She was right. They were furious. How could she muddy the good Gienap name with an unwanted pregnancy? Normally when this happened, a family would send the daughter away to relatives and put the baby up for adoption. But Grandma told her parents that she and Levi wanted to get married. She thought her parents would be relieved. Levi was a member of a prominent family in the community, had his own farm, and Grandma loved him and his four children.

But her father, Herman, was frank and belligerent with his daughter. He let her know that she was disowned. He vowed he would never again speak to her or her children. This must have been heart-breaking for a young woman who had always loved and admired her papa. But that sentiment didn't stop her.

On December 1, 1916, the *Daily Freeman Tribune* reported:

> Two well-known Webster City residents; Miss Gertrude Gienap, daughter of Herman and Martha Gienap and Mr. Levi Cottington of Stratford, son of Mr. and Mrs. Levi Cottington, Sr., were quietly married at the University parsonage. The Reverend Harry B. Shook officiated. The young people were accompanied by the brother of the bride, Walter Gienap. The congratulations and well wishes of their friends will be extended them for a happy and prosperous wedded life.

Walter was the only guest to attend the wedding. Although, Grandma's father had disowned her, the Cottington family welcomed her with open arms. Shortly after the wedding, my grandparents quietly moved 70 miles north to a 360-acre farm in Forest City, Iowa to start a new life. About five months later, their son, Keith was born on May 17. They were suddenly a family of seven.

When one is looking into the family history, you sometimes find sorrow and tragedy and you marvel at the resilience and strength of your family members. Other times there are odd and funny twists and turns. I was heart-broken that Grandma's papa treated her in that manner. Herman was true to his word, and he never saw or spoke again to his daughter or his thirteen grandchildren, and he wrote Grandma out of his will. Grandma did make peace with her mother, who was known as very mild, quiet, and obedient to her husband. However, whenever Grandma came to see her, Herman would run out of the house and busy himself in his wood-working shop. He never wanted to meet those precious children.

With an aching curiosity, I kept researching Great-grandpa Herman Gienap, and sure enough, found some irony. When I finally found his marriage certificate, I discovered he was married on December 14, 1892, and their first child, Walter, was born on July 20, 1893—seven months later. Oh, the irony!

THE EMERGING AGE OF AUTO AND AIR TRANSPORTATION

In the emerging era of auto transportation in the first couple of decades of the twentieth century, hundreds of small companies across the country were building motor cars and thousands of people were buying their first car. The famous auto magnate, Henry Ford, first gained fame as an auto racer rather than a manufacturer, when in 1904, he set a new motor car land speed record of ninety-four mph. He continued to experiment with the car, and finally in 1908, his first Model T Ford rolled off the assembly line. Over the next nineteen years, the Ford Motor Company sold 15 million Model T cars.

One fellow in Iowa was particularly intrigued with Henry Ford and his new Model T Ford. Clyde Herring was an entrepreneur who resided in Atlantic, Iowa, a charming town nestled alongside the East Nishnabotna River, eighty miles west of the state capital of Des Moines. In his past, Clyde had tinkered in a number of professions, including jewelry repair in Michigan, ranching in Colorado, and farming in Massena, Iowa, but he wanted to do more with his life. According to a 1935 article in *Time* magazine, Clyde first met Henry Ford when he fixed Ford's watch back in Clyde's Michigan days. Based on this brief meeting, the clever Clyde decided he would write the famous carmaker and see if he could get a Ford Model T at a wholesale price. Bold move.

But the irascible and unpredictable Ford, immediately wrote two letters back to Clyde: one appointing Clyde as a Ford dealer in Atlantic, and the other letter from a railroad agency informing Clyde there were three Ford Model Ts waiting for him at the Atlantic railroad station. Clyde quickly sold two of the Fords for a $300 profit and kept the third—at wholesale price. Clyde had found his calling and became one of the top Ford dealers in the country. His Atlantic Automobile Company building featured elaborate chandeliers, huge plate glass windows and potted plants. He developed more locations and then moved his operations to Des Moines.

Clyde and Ford grew so close that in 1916, Clyde managed to talk Ford into building a Ford assembly plant in Des Moines. In 1920, the new Ford plant, located on the corner of 19th and Grand Avenue, was finished at a cost of $420,000, and survives today as a center for college and technical courses in the Des Moines Public School District. But Clyde's story doesn't end there. In the 1930s, Clyde became only the second Democrat in Iowa to serve as governor, and in 1936, he won a US Senate seat.

In addition to automobiles, this period was also a time of development for the airplane. The Wright Brothers were credited with inventing, building, and flying the world's first successful motor operated airplane. Their first sustained flight was on December 17, 1903, south of Kitty Hawk, North Carolina. The brothers were awarded a contract in 1908 to establish the world's first flying school in France. In 1909, they completed proving flights for the US Army, and created an aircraft holding two people that remained aloft for an entire hour. The armed forces may have not realized it at the time, but the new flying machines would become a crucial fighting force in the country's upcoming wars.

WORLD WAR I AND THE PANDEMIC

World War I was declared in July 1914 and lasted until November, 1918. Some estimates indicate that worldwide, up to 40 million soldiers and civilians were killed or wounded in the war. The US yearned to stay out of the war, but a series of German attacks eventually convinced the US to get involved. On May 7, 1915, a German U-boat torpedoed the British-owned steamship *Lusitania*, killing 1,195 souls, including 118 Americans. After Germany executed a number of additional submarine attacks on passenger and merchant ships, President Woodrow Wilson, on April 2, 1917, went before a joint session of Congress to request a declaration of war against Germany.

After the declaration of war, Grandma's brother, Walter, dutifully joined the army and had to leave his dear fiancée. The army soon determined that Walter had flat feet and was honorably discharged. Walter came marching flat-footed home to find that his fiancée had married someone else. The kind and decent Walter held a lasting torch for his ex-fiancée and never married. Despite this, Walter led a long, prosperous life and inherited all of his father's farms and wealth. Both of Grandma's sisters became teachers and "spinsters." Alice lived much of her life with Walter in the farmhouse built by their father in 1901. Grandma remembered when she was a six-year-old, pushing her doll carriage and all her dolls into the beautiful new home.

Sometime in the 1960s, Grandma took me to visit her childhood home and meet Walter and Alice. I thought the beautiful farmhouse was a mansion. Inside there was a stunning dining room filled with flowing velvet draperies, Waterford crystal, bone china, Hummel figurines, and exotic souvenirs from Alice and Esther's many trips all over the world. The entire house was filled with Great-grandpa Herman's beautiful home-crafted furniture. Things I had never seen in my life. Years later, in 1976, Walter went to the basement to light the pilot light on the furnace, and it exploded in his face. Walter and Alice managed to rush out of the house, but it burned to the ground, with all its treasures melting in the heat. Walter was rushed to the hospital in Fort Dodge and died within days. Alice was so traumatized by the event that she was admitted to a nursing home and died within a few months. We never know how life will turn out.

In March of 1918, with the country enmeshed in war, outbreaks of a flu-like illness were first detected in the United States, when more than 100 soldiers at Camp Funston in Fort Riley, Kansas became ill with a strange flu. Within two years, nearly a third of the global population, or an estimated 500 million people, were infected in four successive waves of variants of the flu. By May of 1918, hundreds of thousands of our soldiers traveled across the Atlantic, and thousands caught the raging flu. According to the book, *Pandemic 1918*, of the 100,000-plus American WWI casualties from battle and other causes, 40,000 died from the "Spanish Flu."

The symptoms of the Spanish or Swine Flu were brutal. Patients developed a high fever, turned blue from lack of oxygen, had coughing fits, and experienced grizzly, projectile bleeding, frothing from their lungs. Sometimes the blood appeared black. Scientists all over the world were racing to investigate the cause of the influenza in an effort to create a vaccine, a form of inoculation that became increasingly common following the pioneer work of Louis Pasteur in 1881. The flu was assumed to be caused by a bacterial disease, but it wasn't until the 1930s that a virus proved to be the cause of the epidemic. There was nothing people could do to fight the pandemic as there were few established treatments other than letting the flu run its course.

Prominent people from all over the world struggled with the disease. India's Mahatma Gandhi caught the flu following the death of his daughter-in-law and his grandson. For religious reasons, he refused any treatment and seemed to be at death's door, but he survived. Sir Arthur Conan Doyle, creator of the famous Sherlock Holmes mysteries, had a son who recovered from severe war wounds, only to succumb to the Spanish Flu. The writer John Steinbeck had the flu so bad, the doctor opened his chest under ether, removed a rib, and drained the infected lung of the pleural pus. The writer Thomas Wolfe in his book, *Look Homeward Angel*, wrote a spellbinding and compelling account of his brother's death from the flu. The famous painter, Gustave Klimt, developed the flu following a stroke in 1918 and died a few months later. During the Paris peace talks in 1919, President Wilson was reputed to have the Spanish Flu when he took ill and fainted during the talks.

During the summer of 1918, the flu in Iowa was getting worse and Grandma was increasingly worried, not only for her five young children, but also because she was pregnant again and due in November. The Iowa Health Department records show that 93,000 Iowans had been infected with the flu, resulting in 6,500 deaths. The peak of the epidemic was in the fall of 1918, when 4.7 million American soldiers came marching home at the end of World War I. Parades were held in major cities as people celebrated the end of the war in the middle of a pandemic. After looking at the old pictures of the parades with hundreds, maybe thousands of people packed together celebrating, I didn't notice too many face masks or any social distancing.

It appeared that rather than a lot of federal and state mandates, each town or city was tasked with decisions on quarantines and closing public facilities. For example, on October 10, 1918, *The Des Moines Register* announced, "Des Moines goes under quarantine today," as the city mandated mask wearing and closing public facilities and schools. The military hospital, Camp Dodge, just a few miles north of Des Moines, was a hot spot with 3,000 ill soldiers, prostrate with the flu. Local workers were going back and forth on public street cars to the camp and people were worried about the workers transmitting the disease back to Des Moines. In the next few months, the city went back and forth on quarantine notices, but the city returned to normal by the spring of 1919. It was estimated there were 675,000 US deaths from the flu, about .006 percent of the population. Nearly a century later, the

2022 COVID-19 pandemic caused over one million US deaths, about .003 percent of the population, even though we had vaccines, mask mandates, massive business shut-downs, and modern hospitals.

The flu was not just limited to the cities of Iowa, but spread throughout the state's rural areas. According to the book, *The Great Influenza*, the most vulnerable victims of the flu were young adults and especially hard hit were pregnant women. During the fall peak of the Spanish Flu, Grandma, pregnant with her second child, Pauline, developed a high fever with coughing fits. Sometimes she turned blue from lack of oxygen. The local doctor came to check on her and announced that she had the flu and needed to be isolated. He didn't want her in the hospital for fear of spreading the disease and besides they couldn't do much anyway, because bed rest and liquids were the only treatments. Grandpa dropped everything, put on a mask, and spent days by her bedside. When Grandma started expelling dark blood from her lungs, the doctor told Grandpa she was near the end.

Grandpa was bereft. In the last five years he had lost his first wife, his mother, and now the doctor was preparing him not only for the death of his new wife, but also the death of their unborn child. For the first time in his life, he questioned the fairness of his God. How much tragedy could he take? For a man who always thought hard work and integrity would be rewarded, he now felt alone and uninspired in this unfair and war-torn world. But he kept praying and asking God to save the life of the mother of his six children. God answered his prayers.

On November 3, 1918, Grandma had recovered from the flu, and gave birth to her daughter, Pauline. Grandpa Levi could finally breathe a sigh of relief as the pandemic was dissipating and Grandma and their six children were alive and well.

THE VAGABONDS

While the war was raging in Europe, America fell more in love with the motor car. In 1900, a trip of 120 miles in one day would have been impossible since there were few drivable roads and horses hitched to a wagon couldn't travel that distance in one day. With the exception of train travel, the average American rarely ventured more than twelve miles from home because that was the round-trip distance a horse and wagon could comfortably cover in a day. The motor car grew by lightning speed. In 1910, there were about 500,000 passenger cars registered in America, however, by 1920 the number had exploded to 8 million cars. After road improvements in the 1920s, the number of registered passenger cars reached over 23 million by 1930.

Most of the travel in this era was through the eastern part of the US, which had the best roads. Millions of people hit the roads with their new motor cars, finally free to go where they wanted, when they wanted. For the first time, the average American could get around and see the sights, just like the wealthy were able to do. This new symbol of independence and personal safety was particularly appreciated by the Black population in this country, who didn't feel safe or well-treated on any public transportation system. The rise in affordability of the motor car allowed Black families to feel safer and have more control of their travels. As the popularity of cars increased, Black families relied on travel guides like the *Green Book*, to help them find safe Black-owned hotels, restaurants, and other facilities.

This new era of "sightseeing" produced a new way of traveling and a whole new vernacular. "Gypsying" became an early popular term for weekend travelers who camped in their cars, and "autocampers" were people who took extended trips, sleeping in or near their cars. Parker Brothers even invented a new game called "Touring," where players navigated their way through flat tires, burned out bearings, thrown rods, detours, and storms that stood in the way of reaching their destination.

Cities and towns everywhere, hoping to attract more tourist dollars, quickly opened autocamps to accommodate the new travelers. Typically, the camps were located near the center of town close to restaurants, shops, and car services. Many of the camps had shower and laundry facilities, central kitchens with all the amenities, electricity, and other accoutrements that tourists demanded. By the 1920s, there were about 4,000 autocamps around the country. However, by the early 1930s most of the autocamps had been closed. The Depression and the Dust Bowl erased the trend of middle-class autocamping and instead bred the creation of homeless camps. By the end of the 1930s, FBI director J. Edgar Hoover, was warning Americans that the new home of crime was the autocamps, where people "risked a brush with disease, bribery, corruption, crookedness, rape, white slavery, thievery, and murder."

The father and P.T. Barnum of the autocamping movement was undoubtedly Henry Ford. He loved to drive the roads and evaluate their quality, hike in the woods, and see the countryside. But Ford was not just a tourist, he was really promoting the concept of buying a car and camping with your family. The "family" who traveled with him were the beloved inventor, Thomas Edison, tire tycoon Harvey Firestone, and naturalist John Burroughs. They dubbed themselves "The Vagabonds."

Ford's main purpose of the summer trips was to demonstrate how much these famous men had in common with other Americans, showing little self-awareness that they actually traveled like the wealthy and sometimes Ford's 200-foot yacht, *Sialia*, was on stand-by near the trips.

Henry Ford and Thomas Edison met at an electronics convention in 1896. Edison was convinced the future was in electric powered cars and encouraged Ford to keep trying to produce electric cars. They became lifelong friends, inspired each other, and formed a common bond around the evils of Wall Street and the crass men who cared only for profit and not for the good of the average American. Neither man had a college degree, and they were disdainful of those who believed classroom education was better than hands-on work experience.

Edison not only invented the first commercially practical incandescent light, but he also created the most efficient generator system to light them. However, he never figured out how to monetize his inventions in the commercial market, even though he possessed a record 1,084 patents. Ford and Edison were loyal friends, but Ford later commented that "Edison is easily the world's greatest scientist, but he is also the world's worst businessman. He knows nothing of business." Edison lyrically described Ford as "an ever-flowing fountain of energy, with a vivid and boundless imagination, instinctive knowledge of mechanisms, and a talent for organization."

Henry Ford met Harvey Firestone in 1905. In Firestone's memoir, *Men and Rubber*, he revealed that in 1905 he heard Ford planned to manufacture 2,000 cars that would sell for $500 each. He figured that was a good market and approached Ford, offering him tires for $55 a set, outbidding the $70 offered by competitors. Firestone realized early that the solid rubber wheels utilized on early cars would not hold up on America's rough roads, so he started offering pneumatic auto tires similar to bike tires, with inflatable inner tubes that helped cushion rides on bumpy roads.

Firestone's tires also sported straight rather than rounded sides, and a deep, wide tread for better traction on all kinds of roads. Firestone had a superior product, but no distribution until he walked into Ford's office. Ford and Firestone became life-long friends and bonded with a shared philosophy: They disdained planned obsolescence, and believed customer loyalty was forged by reasonable prices and long-lasting products. They both felt the most efficient and loyal employees were inspired by higher wages and profit sharing. When Ford set up his auto plant, the normal manufacturing wages were $2 a day for five, ten-hour days. Ford shocked the manufacturing community when he started his workers at $5 a day for five, eight-hour days. People came far and wide for this opportunity, including a large number of Southern Blacks, yearning for a better life.

While planning for one of the Vagabond's first trips in 1913, Ford convinced the group to take a nature hiking trip in New York. Ford chose John Burroughs, the famous naturalist, who had just come back from a wilderness camping trip in Yellowstone National Park with President Theodore Roosevelt, as their guide. Burrough's writings on these trips inspired an entire nation into visiting the magnificent park. Steeped in the theories espoused by Emerson and Thoreau, Burroughs looked forward to taking the famous Edison and Ford on a nature trip. However, this was no ordinary camping trip.

Ford arrived with a fleet of cars loaded with servants and equipment. They had electric lights from portable storage batteries, a chef that prepared spectacular food, and staff to keep their clothes freshly ironed. Not only that, but Ford had all his car dealers on the route to promote the trip and assure that a bastion of reporters would show up at each stop to report on all the antics of the famous Vagabonds. Ford also brought along his own cameramen to record the escapades and sent the films to movie theaters for inclusion in the newsreels that preceded motion pictures. The theaters and the audience ate them up.

Everyone had their role on the Vagabond trips. Ford paid for and organized the trips, fixed the cars when they broke down, and organized contests with the group. Firestone, as a willing lieutenant, took care of the details, coordinated the schedule, and explored around for the best food. Burroughs was in charge of leading the nature hikes and Edison was the navigator guiding the trip, but he mostly pondered his next invention. Although Ford and Edison were the popular draw, all the Vagabonds benefited from the publicity exposure.

The Vagabonds, left to right: Edison, Burroughs, Ford, and Firestone.
Photo courtesy of the Henry Ford Collection

As exciting as the era was, the "Golden Age of Farming and Transportation" was about to change dramatically in the next couple of decades.

CHAPTER THREE

THE 1920S ON AN IOWA FARM

ON NOVEMBER 2, 1920, GRANDMA TUCKED HER THREE-MONTH-OLD SON, MY FATHER, RICHARD, UNDER HER ARMS AND PROCEEDED TO DRIVE INTO THE COUNTY SEAT, FOREST CITY, LEAVING THE SIX OTHER CHILDREN AT HOME WITH GRANDPA. My dad was breast feeding, so he needed to come along. Grandma was a woman on a mission. This was the first time she was allowed to vote and she supported all the freedoms for which women were fighting. She entered the building and headed toward the poll booth, but stopped cold in mid-step. She noticed a small group of older Iowa farm men in coveralls, thumbs tightly wound around the coverall straps, resting in chairs gathered around an old-fashioned pot-bellied stove. Their conversation came to an abrupt halt when they realized what Grandma was about to do. Oh my god, she's going to vote! The first woman to do so in Winnebago County.

Grandma, a steely pioneer woman, who eventually raised thirteen children, was an equal partner in running the family farm. She had seen it all, but this encounter was making her a little nervous. Would these old farmers try to prevent her from voting? She knew a number of men in the county were vehemently opposed to women voting. After all, women would just vote the way their husbands told them, so why bother? As she nervously signed in and received her ballot, one of the farmers was heard to pronounce, "Well, if Gertrude is going to vote, we might as well go home and get our wives up here to vote, too." They got up from their chairs and ambled out the door. Grandma was relieved and pleased that she inspired the men to get their wives out to vote.

THE IOWA FARM IN THE 1920S

My grandparents worked a well-run 360-acre farm just outside of Forest City, Iowa. They had both come from a long line of successful farmers, so they understood the essentials of farming: Never get into serious debt, work day and night, diversify your crops and animals to preserve the soil, raise the products that would have the best pricing, help your neighbors, go to church every Sunday, and . . . pray a lot about the weather, storms, crop prices, bugs, health of the animals, and a million other details. There was potential calamity everywhere.

There was a lot for farmers to pray about in the 1920s. The Golden Age of Agriculture, flush with war-time government subsidies and high demand, kept farm prices up during and shortly after WWI, but very quickly, things changed dramatically. The federal government withdrew price supports and many farm and crop prices were cut in half. In some cases, commodity prices barely covered the costs of production. Between 1921 and 1929, thousands of farmers who had invested heavily in the war-time growth, were now having problems covering their costs and paying their bank loans. Foreclosures were common and that affected the health of the community banks. There were about 214,000 farms in Iowa, with an average size of 156 acres. In that era, 95 percent of all the land in Iowa was involved in farming. Between 1921 and 1931, about half the farms were near bankruptcy and, according to the Federal Reserve and the *Annals of Iowa*, the state of Iowa led the nation with 870 bank failures. In 1900, land in Iowa averaged about $43 an acre, but by 1920, the price had rocketed to $227 an acre. When price supports were dropped and the Depression dragged on, farmland pummeled downward to $78 an acre by 1940, and half the farms in the state were managed by tenants, not owners.

If you are unfamiliar with Iowa farmers, you might think they were just simple tillers of the soil. But they were more like Renaissance people and the stewardship of farming lived deep in their soul. They had to be students of crop and soil science and understand the methods of production and marketing, crop and pest control, and soil conservation. They had to be astute businesspeople, understanding the business principles of debt, cost controls, and the economic ups and downs of crop and animal prices. They needed to stay alert about the uncontrollable devastation caused by politics and the weather. They knew how to construct and repair buildings, silos, and fences. They knew how to operate and repair the most complex farm machinery and understood the principles of the care and feeding of numerous animals.

Fortunately, my grandparents had kept their debts low, had savings, and thought they could weather the storm during the ravages of the 1920s. Their farm was anchored by a large, two-story farmhouse, with plenty of room for the big, growing family. However, as with most farmhouses in that time period, it was not insulated or heated on the second story. There were no storm doors or insulated windows, but there were screens for the summer. The house was drafty and cold in the winter and stifling hot in the summer. There was a three-acre grove of trees north of the house that provided a windbreak from the brutal Iowa winters. However, you still needed a mound of home-made quilts at night to develop a modicum of warmth.

The urban dwellers had it much better. Many people who lived in cities around the country in the 1920s had electricity, central heating, refrigerators, electrical appliances, and other conveniences. However, the average farm in Iowa and around the country did not have any of that technology. Rural electrification didn't appear until the late 1930s. However, Grandpa was an early adopter and in the early 1920s installed electric wiring in the house, run by a gas generator and batteries, which provided lighting for the home. There were no fireplaces in the house or any central heating and certainly no air-conditioning. There was a coal furnace in the cellar, which heated the living room through a grate in the floor, and the kitchen was heated by the cookstove. The upstairs bedrooms were frigidly cold in the winter.

The kitchen was the gathering place and the heart of the home. It was furnished with a wooden pantry and other wooden cabinets, a large kitchen table, and a ponderous cast iron stove. There was an indoor pump by the kitchen sink, so they didn't have to carry water from the well into the kitchen. Near the sink was a large wooden cabinet, with two built-in, tin-lined bins that pulled out to hold fifty pounds of flour in one bin and twenty-five pounds of sugar in the other. There was a heavily enameled shelf that pulled out so you could roll out a piecrust or mix a cake.

The large, black, cast-iron cookstove was fueled by dried corn cobs and wood. There were four large stove lids plus one small lid on the top of the stove. One could tilt the lids with a detachable handle and throw in the corn cobs. The oven door folded down to insert baked goods. Heavy cast iron skillets were used to cook or fry on top of the stove. A large reservoir for water was attached to the right-hand side, filled with soft water from the cistern for dish washing and bathing. So how could they bring the temperature of the oven up and down, when the stove was heated by piles of burning corn cobs and wood? They filled a kettle of water and carefully poured it into the reservoir until it achieved the appropriate temperature for whatever they were baking—savory home-made pies, roasts, cookies, cakes, and Grandma's fabulous homemade bread and cinnamon buns. I still dream about those lard-laden foods, with fresh hand-grown ingredients.

There was no electric washing machine—Grandma used a wooden wash tub, with a washboard, and a hand-operated clothes wringer. There was no dryer, so all the clothes had to be hung on the massive clothesline in the backyard. Clothes that needed to be ironed were taken off the line when they were dry, sprinkled with a little water, and rolled up to wait for ironing the next day. The iron was a heavy piece of cast iron that was heated on top of the stove. It must have been hard not to burn yourself.

By 1920, more than 70 percent of the farms in Illinois, Iowa, Kansas, and Nebraska had telephones, typically installed by independent, private telephone coops that grew rapidly in the Midwest. The phones were on a "party line," so you had to wait your turn. When the others got done talking, you could ring the operator and ask for your party. I would guess that nearly every party line in the Midwest had a few old souls who wanted to yak all day and wouldn't get off the phone. It was a frustrating system that lasted until the 1970s in some rural communities. Although some from the rural areas got their news from the party line, most farmers in Iowa heard their news from Iowa State College's WOI radio station on their battery-operated radios. They also depended on Iowa State's extension services and the *Chicago Daily Drovers' Journal*, to learn the latest in agriculture, pricing, weather, and world events.

My grandparents had a number of other buildings scattered within walking distance of the main house. They were very proud of the barn they built in 1920, the year my father was born. These large barns were essential as they provided shelter for the cattle and horses, storage for hay, grain, plows, tools, and a small corn crib. The second level of the barn was used for hay storage. There was usually a rope and pulley that made it easier to haul hay to the second level. The barn, built in 1920, served as a metaphor for the agricultural dividing line between the age of prosperity and the age of despair.

In addition to the barn, there were chicken coops, pig pens, a windmill, and a silo. A silo is a tall, narrow, air-tight building for storing

The 1920 barn built by Grandpa

grain or fermented feed known as silage. It keeps the silage succulent and slightly sour so it's edible for farm animals. My grandparents were committed to learning about good farming techniques like straightening creek and river channels to recover land for cultivation or pasturing, crop rotation, and other techniques they learned from the Iowa State extension services.

The most important animals on the farm were the draft horses and the cows. The draft horses, weighing 1,400 to 2,000 pounds each, were used for the hardest of labor. They plowed the ground, brought in the hay crop, pulled wagons of field corn to town, pulled cars out of the mud, and hauled manure. The cows produced the milk and also were butchered for meat. Pigs and hogs were good money-makers, but the animals were said to have the intelligence of a three-year-old, so they were always up to something.

There were two ways to collect water on the farm: a windmill to pump water from an underground aquifer, pond, or river, and a cistern to collect soft rainwater. The windmill, powered by wind and sometimes by a gasoline engine, pumped water into a large tank. There was a short pipe sticking out from the top of the tank, so when water trickled out, you knew it was time to take the windmill out of gear to stop pumping.

Farmers generally depended on the wind for power, but when the wind died down, they used a small, noisy gasoline-powered engine to pump the water for livestock.

The second way of getting water was collecting and storing rainwater in a cistern, which was usually thirty-to forty-feet deep and lined with stones. Rainwater, unlike well water, is soft and allows suds to form so it is good for bathing and washing clothes. Well water was used for drinking and cooking because it tasted good and made good coffee.

My grandparents had a windmill that pumped water from the well into a large tank. They had an unusual arrangement where the water from the tank was pumped into a pipe that traversed through a small concrete building and then out to the feeding troughs for the animals. The concrete building was called an "ice house" and had no windows and only one small door. The cold water in the pipes kept the ice house cold enough that they could keep home-made pies fresh on the shelves.

There was also an underground root cellar to store vegetables for the winter and an underground storage space for coal. The house had a large basement which held shelves for canned goods, room for the kids to play in the winter, and a coal furnace that heated the living room.

There was an established routine for all the chores. Monday was wash day, Tuesday was ironing, and Saturday was bath day. Marilee remembered bath day, "Mother would heat the boiler full of water and then pour it in a big tub set in front of the stove, surrounded by chairs covered in blankets for privacy and warmth. The oldest boys went first and then the water was changed for the girls, allowing the oldest girls to bathe first. I didn't have my first bath in a real tub with fresh, clean water until we moved to Bode in 1939—at the age of ten." On Saturday night everyone got dressed up and went to town to visit friends, see a movie, or go to a dance. Sunday was reserved for church and church dinners.

Every day, even when the snow was deep and the feeding troughs frozen, the animals needed to be fed, cows needed to be milked, and milk and eggs gathered for customers. Three meals a day needed to be cooked for the large family plus the hired hands. The family raised, butchered, canned, or cured their own meat and vegetables. They made their own bread and ground their own flour from oats and wheat, bought coffee beans from the general store and hand-ground them in a manual coffee grinder. Grandma made most of their clothes on a Singer sewing machine operated manually with a foot treadle. She crocheted and knitted sweaters, scarves, and socks and made quilts and rag rugs, using remnants from old clothes. She made soap out of the fat from pigs and hogs. Everything was used and reused; nothing was wasted. Most Iowa farmers lived by the motto, "Use it up, wear it out, make it do, or do without."

Everyone on the farm had their own jobs. Grandpa would plow the fields with the large draft horses and a manual steel plow. He decided what to plant and when to plant it, harvested and cultivated the crops, and drove wagons full of crops into town. Grandpa was also in charge of finances and negotiating with his local bank, the Farmer's Savings Bank in Leland. During the 1920s and early 1930s, my grandparents hired a farm hand and his wife to help out with the chores. The help was essential because in 1920, there were seven children, the oldest of which was only fourteen. During the 1920s, Grandma had four more children: Gwen, Rex, Bruce, and Marilee and two more children in the 1930s: Barbara and Levi III.

Grandma managed the house, the chicken coops, pig pens, gardens, and all the household chores. During the tough times in the 1920s and 30s, these small animals and the gardens would produce nearly half of the income of the farm. Women were indeed equal partners. All the children were expected to work. Even the smallest kids could make their beds, collect eggs, pick and wash fruit and vegetables, carry wood and water, wash and dry dishes, and gather berries and apples. Older children could drive a tractor or plow, harness and drive the horses, pull weeds out of the crops, feed the pigs and chickens, care for the smaller children, and plant, pick, and can fruit and vegetables.

This is a world unimaginable to much of the youth today. Everyone woke up at the crack of dawn and worked hard all day. There were no iPads or iPhones, no television or video games, no electricity nor running water. Most farms didn't have central heating, relying instead on stoves or fireplaces. There was no indoor bathroom, just the famous wooden outhouse, with the ubiquitous Sears catalog available for wiping or reading. Every year the outhouse was moved to a new location and the old hole filled to hide the smell. Marilee remarked that, "In a bad winter, the parents would let the kids do their duty on a newspaper and then throw it into the furnace fire."

All the children attended a country schoolhouse, down the street from their farm home. Marilee, a teacher herself, commented, "Country schools typically had only twenty to thirty neighborhood students and the teachers had a hard life and were not paid well. There was no electricity or indoor plumbing, so the teacher had to go to school early to start the fire in the wood stove so it would be warm when the kids arrived. The teacher was also responsible for keeping the inside of the building clean, the children were responsible for the yard." Their school was about twenty by twenty feet, wood frame, with a couple of windows on each side. There was a large pole with a flag outside and a swing set for recess.

The same attitude toward industriousness and diligence that applied to chores, was reinforced in the one-room schoolhouse. Lunches were carried in the dinner pails filled with sandwiches of homemade bread and meat, wrapped in paper. Teachers taught all eight grades and older students would help teach the younger ones. Every student had a wooden desk with a hole in the upper right-hand corner to hold a bottle of ink for their ink pens. Left-handed children were chastised to fit into society and use their right hand. Most schools had an upright piano sitting in a corner, a large American flag on a pole, and a pot-bellied stove for warmth.

Although country doctors were available for an emergency, most issues could be solved with home remedies. If you had a bee sting, you would apply baking soda, black mud, or earwax to remove the pain. If you had a canker sore, you would chew on a green pepper. Every home had Vaseline, lard, baking soda, boric acid, salt, camphor, hydrogen peroxide, Vicks Mentholatum, tincture of iodine, and Mercurochrome.

Women had their babies at home with little help and it was a painful and dangerous experience.

The schedule for the year was carefully orchestrated. In the spring, the farmers would borrow money from the bank to buy seeds for planting. There were two types of crops—cash crops sold in the fall for cash and crops used to feed the animals. Every spring, baby chicks in cardboard cartons, were delivered by mail. It was cheaper and more convenient to buy the chicks, rather than incubate them from a small egg.

One of the biggest issues in the spring was the ubiquitous Iowa mud, which was created by the depth of the winter frost, the amount of spring rain, and how much dirt the animals had stirred up. The mud could be ankle or knee high and was especially troublesome if you had to drive to town on muddy roads. The chickens and pigs managed well in the mud, but deep mud caked the cows' udders, chapping their tender teats. One of the trickiest jobs in the spring was rubbing Bag Balm on those tender teats. Don't stand behind the cow, they do kick!

Gardening officially began sometime in April, usually with hardier crops like potatoes. In April and May, they would plant onions, peas, yellow wax beans, radishes, sweet corn, lettuce, tomatoes, cabbage, and pepper plants in the large garden near the house.

In northern Iowa, the average late spring frost of the season was about May 15. About a month before that date, you could plant trees and shrubs, perennial flowers and herbs, roses and cool seasonal flowers like pansies, and cool seasonal vegetables like parsley, radishes, and spinach. Soybeans were planted in June and ripened in October. Wheat grew well in the Midwest, but it lacked a regional market and local grain elevators typically specialized only in corn. Midwest wheat farmers could not compete with farmers on the Great Plains, who benefitted from economies of scale.

Corn was planted in May, and by the first of June it was a few inches high. Corn was cultivated four times before it was tall and leafy enough to outcompete the weeds. Row cultivation for corn can encourage root development by breaking the surface soil, encouraging better soil aeration, and reducing puddles of water. Horses could plow about two-to-three acres a day, so it could take a while to plow and plant a large farm. One of the most time-saving inventions for farmers was the tractor and it caught on fast. By 1930, there were a million gas-powered tractors working on farms in this country.

By mid-June, the strawberries and cherries were ripening and Grandma was busy canning and making strawberry jam. July produced blackberries, raspberries, and hollyhocks. Starting in August, the apples were ready, and Grandma busied herself making applesauce and apple pies. Men worked on hay in July and cut rye, barley, and oats. It was imperative to get the hay cut, dried, and into the barns between rainstorms.

Threshing was the main activity for the men in August. Traveling men with threshing machines with gas engines went from farm to farm to feed bundles of grain into the thresher to separate the grain from the chaff and straw. They would stay for a few days and typically sleep in the barn. Grandma would provide all the meals. Grandma had cooked hundreds of meals for farm hands and generally they were very appreciative. However, one day a hungry farm hand stormed into her kitchen and demanded Grandma make him dinner—right now! She calmly told him, "You have a choice: you can hold the baby or cook the food yourself." The man had the deer-in-the-headlights look of someone who had never held a baby, cooked a meal, or had a woman speak to him like that. Grandma handed him the baby and prepared his meal. Grandma later confessed to us that she often held a baby and cooked a meal at the same time; but only for people who showed a little respect.

In mid-September, corn was dry and usually ready to cut. In northwest Iowa, the first frost of the winter could be as early as late September. Grandma and the kids would pick the tomatoes, beets, grapes, peaches, cucumbers, and crabapples, and start the canning process. One of the keys to this process was the new Ball Ideal Mason canning jar which first appeared around 1915. The jars were clear glass with effective seals that kept the food fresh nearly all winter in the cellar. Beets, cucumbers, and crabapples were pickled, and grapes turned into juice. At some point, the kids would collect honey from the nearby beehives. This was a carefully crafted art.

Fall was also the time of year for dressing the roosters and butchering the hogs. Roosters were hung upside down, heads decapitated, and blood drained. The bodies were dipped in hot water so the feathers would be easier to pull out. The process stunk to high heavens, but you weren't done yet. The legs were cut off and the organs and intestines removed. The meat was chilled until it was time to cook or freeze. A dreadful process, but the fried chicken and fresh-cooked corn on the cob made it all worthwhile.

Hogs were shot with a .22 rifle, their throats cut and bled out, and bodies scalded in hot water. Hogs have a thick layer of fat just under the skin, so they are hard to skin. After skinning, the carcass is dismembered, and the lard poured into five-gallon containers for storage. Lard was the staple for good cooking. The ham from the hogs would be cured in a salty brine solution and hung in the smoke house. Cattle were usually taken to a professional butcher to kill and process.

By October, the corn husking and hay baling were completed. Plowing had to be done before the ground froze hard. The cornstalks were cut, bound, and set up in the fields in September. In October, the stalks were fed into a shredder, powered by a steam engine. The corn and grain were stored in bins. When prices seemed fair, they would haul the crops and animals to town.

In November, the shredding and corn husking occupied much of the month. In late fall the men would patch holes and cracks and make repairs on the barn, hog, and chicken houses, to help protect the animals from the brutal winter.

The cool weather in the fall brought hormonal level changes in the animals that increased the "drive" that resulted in spring calving or lambing. Birthing in the spring, rather than the winter, helped the animals grow and thrive. The shorter gestation period of pigs and sheep made it natural to breed in the fall with birthing in the spring. A pig is a young swine that is not yet mature. A hog is over three years old and weighs more than 120 pounds.

Although some of this may seem like a bucolic and nostalgic glimpse of the past, farming was a difficult and complex life. There were many dangers that lurked in every corner of the farm. Flammable kerosene lamps were dangerous and dim. There were a number of gas- or steam-powered machines with sharp blades, open belts, and dangerous augers. Animal behavior was also unpredictable and dangerous. Diseases like typhoid fever, whooping cough, diphtheria, infant death, tuberculosis, cancer, pneumonia, measles, scarlet fever, rickets, and others, did not have advanced treatments available. The silos sometimes held deadly gas build up. The weather was threatening all year long from blizzards and ice storms in the winter to tornadoes and floods the rest of the year.

In addition to this complex life, was another hardship—crop prices had tanked, and it was hard to make a profit. The USDA national price index of farm products was started in 1899 with an index of 100. By 1920, the golden age of farming had doubled the index to 205, but by 1927, the index had taken a terrible toboggan slide down to 131. Despite all these hardships, most Iowa farmers considered themselves blessed. Farming was not just a job, but a calling for the entire family and a way to pass on wealth to the next generation.

THE COUNTY SEAT TOWN

The nearby towns were important to farmers and the social center of their lives. My grandparents lived just a couple of miles from the town of Forest City, the county seat of Winnebago County, near the Minnesota border. The city was platted in 1856, incorporated in 1878, and by 1920 had a population of about 2,000.

The state of Iowa is divided into townships and Winnebago County has twelve townships. Each township is made up of thirty-six sections, and each section is one square mile, which could be conveniently divided into four farms of 160 acres each. This size acreage was considered a manageable size for a farm in the 1920s, using horse-drawn plows.

The state of Iowa has ninety-nine counties, and each county seat was logistically located in the spot where every member of the county could make a round-trip wagon ride to the county seat in one day. Small towns celebrated their selection as a county seat, because it implied permanency and importance as a town. In the center of a county seat town would be a large square block of beautiful green grass and trees, with an immense courthouse plopped in the middle. Wide streets would surround the courthouse grounds, all lined with important retail stores.

The Winnebago County courthouse was replaced in 1896 with an imposing Romanesque Revival style building of red brick, trimmed with stone. The current structure is three stories high, topped off with a five-story clock tower. The building is capped with a hipped roof surrounded by three projecting pavilions with pyramid shaped roofs. It is an impressive structure important enough to let everyone know Forest City was a town that mattered.

Not far from the courthouse were several churches and banks, a high school, a Ford dealer, a couple of rival hotels owned by rival banks, a movie theater, drug stores, grocery stores, attorney and doctor offices, restaurants, and several retail stores lined up across the street from the courthouse. On the edges of town stood a couple of hospitals, a railroad station, and the ever so important grain elevator. In 1903, the Lutheran church opened a small university called Waldorf University, retrofitted from an abandoned hotel. This small town of only 2,000 citizens had every convenience and necessity that anyone could wish for. It was a wonderful way to live, but a feat difficult for any small town to accomplish today. Currently, Forest City, with a population of 7,150, thrives not only because of the farmers and the university, but also because of Winnebago Industries, a leading manufacturer of motor homes.

The social center of small-town Iowa was the church. Many times, the church dinners were potluck, and each farm wife brought her specialties: baked pies, chocolate cake, fried chicken, potato salad, and other homemade goodies. The church organized sewing bees, auxiliary meetings, and ice cream socials. The biggest events occurred at Christmas, Easter, weddings, baptisms, and funerals. Grandpa preferred to turn to the Universalist Church in Webster City. Dr. Effie McCollum Jones, the pastor there for fifty-five years, was a good friend of the family. She was a nationally recognized suffragist and appointed by Mrs. Carrie Chapman Catt to be a field director for the National Woman Suffrage, barnstorming the country for the right to vote. The *Webster City Daily Freeman* called her "one of Iowa's greatest women leaders in the community, who provided a richer, fuller life for everyone with whom she came in contact."

People in Iowa took Sunday very seriously. Section 5040 of the Iowa General Assembly described the Blue Laws of the day. "If any person . . . engaged in carrying firearms, dancing, hunting, shooting, horse racing or in any way disturbing a worshipping assembly or in buying or selling property . . . shall be fined." Some women in small towns felt that women wearing slacks on Sunday was "verboten," German for "forbidden."

Besides the church, there were a variety of activities in town including county and state fairs, 4H and other clubs, movies, books, radios, and sports. Popular books of the era included T.S. Eliot's *Wasteland* poem, which described the trauma, disillusion, and death after World War I. *Ulysses* by James Joyce explored the process of thinking, F. Scott Fitzgerald's *The Great Gatsby*, cynically dissected the social classes, Franz Kafka's *The Trial*, expressed the growing fears of totalitarian oppression and bureaucracy in the modern world, and Langston Hughes's poem, *Weary Blues*, revealed the power and pain in Black art.

My grandparents were very active in their community including work in the Farm Bureau and the county fair, and Grandpa even starred in a local play called *A Poor Married Man: A Farce Comedy in Three Acts*. Grandma performed in the play, *The Little Blue Teapot*.

While the average Iowa farmer was struggling with the farm depression in the late 1920s, the Ford Motor Company was also struggling with the sinking fortunes of the Model T.

CHAPTER FOUR

1926: YOU'RE AHEAD IN A FORD ALL THE WAY. FROM THE MODEL T TO THE MODEL A

IT WAS 1926 AND THE 10,000 FORD DEALERS AROUND THE COUNTRY WERE IN AN UPROAR. The popular Model T sales were slumping and the competition was grabbing market share. The dealers wanted action now! The new General Motors president, Alfred Sloan, had developed a plan to take market share from Ford, and his plan was working. Sloan knew he couldn't compete with Ford on technical innovation or pricing. He knew innovation was expensive and unpredictable and he couldn't make the cars cheaper than the efficient Ford system. Sloan believed his competitive edge was building craft-built luxury cars with snazzy new features and bright new colors that would appeal to consumers of the go-go Jazz Age. He decided to consolidate many of the disparate GM brands and give them the same basic body, but with annual cosmetic design changes. It worked and within a couple of years, GM had purloined substantial market share from Ford.

Henry Ford, his son Edsel, and the executive team at Ford took the dealers seriously and were immersed in the middle of a raging debate about the future of the trend-setting Model T Ford. After eighteen years of solid growth, sales were down by 450,000 units, while GM's Chevrolet production was up nearly 30 percent. When the first Model T Ford rolled off the assembly lines in 1908, the American public went bananas—with good reason. At that time, there were hundreds of motor car manufacturers in the country that were tediously building their cars by hand, one by one. This process made the cars expensive, unreliable, and costly to maintain. But Henry Ford had a better idea to mass produce cars on an assembly line with completely interchangeable parts, marketed to the middle class at a low price.

Back in 1908, Ford had boldly described his vision for the new Model T Ford:

> I will build a motor car for the great multitudes. It will be large enough for the family, but small enough for the individual to run and care for. It will be constructed of the best materials, by the best men to be hired, after the simplest designs that modern engineering can devise. But it will be so low in price that no man making a good salary will be unable to own one—and enjoy with his family the blessing of hours of pleasure in God's great open spaces.

Ford made industrial history when he invented the 40-hour work week and decided to pay the Model T workers $5 for an eight-hour day, substantially more than the standard $2 for a ten-hour day. Some believe this helped to create a middle class in the Upper Midwest. Between 1910 and 1920, higher wages and available jobs in the Upper Midwest helped create the "Great Migration," when nearly half a million Southern Blacks moved north to take advantage of these opportunities. By the end of World War I, over 8,000 Blacks were working in Detroit's auto industry, and Ford became a leader in hiring Blacks.

The Model T was first tested by Henry Ford himself, who took the vehicle on a hunting trip to Wisconsin to test the workability of the auto's features. The new car was different in many ways. Most cars of the era had the steering wheel on the right side of the car—just like in London. However, Ford decided to move the steering to the left side of the car, so men could drive up to a curb, and safely let their wives out on the sidewalk.

The Model T was unique because it was the first car to have its engine block and crankcase cast as a single unit and the first car to make extensive use of the lightweight but strong alloy known as vanadium steel. This allowed the much-lighter Model T to skim over rock-rutted, pothole-clotted roads that shook heavier cars to pieces. It was easier to shift gears in the car, and it had an option for a windshield. Henry Ford's famous quote, "Any customer can have a car painted any color that he wants so long as it's black," was not quite accurate. Most of the Model Ts were black, because it was the fastest drying color. However, one could also get a variety of colors including blue, red, gray, and green.

The car experienced astounding growth because it was the first affordable car for the average American family. More than 15 million Model Ts, referred to as the "Tin Lizzie", were built and sold. By the early 1920s, more than half of the registered motor cars in the world were Fords. In many ways the "Tin Lizzie" was a metaphor for the innovation and mass production trends that aided and abetted the rise of the middle class.

Ford was able to produce affordable cars not only because of production and mechanical improvements, but also because Ford refused to pay royalties to the Association of Licensed Automobile Manufacturing (ALAM). The ALAM required each car maker to pay a $2,000 entry fee and 1.25 percent royalty for each gas-powered vehicle. Ford applied in 1903, but ALAM turned him down because his two previous car companies had failed. Ford started producing the Model Ts without paying royalties and told ALAM, "sue me." They did and the lawsuits dragged on for years until a 1911 appellate court ruled that no carmakers were required to pay licensing fees.

Ford was very proud of his innovative Model T. He proclaimed often:

> There was no conscious public need of motor cars when we first made [them]. There were few good roads. This car blazed the way for the motor industry and started the movement for good roads everywhere.

Ford steadfastly believed the success of the Model T was due to the service orientation of the local dealers. He often stated:

> Some of the early manufacturers proceeded on the theory that once they had induced a man to buy a car, they had him at their mercy and charged the highest possible price for replacements. Our company adopted the opposite theory. We believed when a man bought one of our cars, we should keep it running for him as long as we could and at the lowest upkeep cost.

But in late 1926, the Ford executives decided the Model T's reign had come to an end. Now there were three tasks to accomplish as quickly as possible: design a new car, retool the factory and assembly plants, and develop a marketing plan . . . in less than one year!

By the end of the year, drawings for the body-layout were begun and the first blueprints were available in January 1927. There were several unique features about the new Model A that made it safer, cheaper to maintain, and easier to drive. By changing the manifold and carburetor, and opening up the passages around the exhaust valve, they were able to gear the car up to forty horsepower. The engine had a quick take-off and one engineer boasted, "the Model A could skin the pants off anything on the road." Henry Ford also insisted the engineers get rid of the fourteen screws holding the carburetor together, and replace them with only one bolt, in order to streamline the process and cut costs.

The Ford executive team moved swiftly and on May 26, 1927, each of the 10,000 Ford dealers in the country received the following telegram from Edsel B. Ford:

> Starting early production entirely new Ford car announcing Thursday new model superior design and performance to any now in low price light car field—STOP—new model has speed style flexibility and control in traffic costlier to manufacture but more economical to operate—STOP—Model T will continue important part of factory production for 10 million owners requiring replacements and service. Under no circumstances are details of the new Ford car to be given out to anyone.

Ford advised the dealers that before the new Model As were available, they should use the time to build up the service and parts departments and do everything they could to find used cars and rebuild them for sale. Regional managers drove to each dealer and helped them with these plans and tried to keep them on board. Normal dealer attrition was about 10 percent, so Ford was relieved when they experienced only 15 percent attrition during the retrofit of the plants.

On the same day the Ford dealers learned about the new Model A, Henry and Edsel Ford drove the 15 millionth Model T out of the factory and shut down the Model T operation. Building the new facility involved retrofitting the old Ford River Rouge complex, as well as overhauling the thirty-four assembly plants in the US and Canada, twelve overseas factories, and numerous shops of independent suppliers. It took only five months at a cost of $250 million to retrofit all the plants. Some experts claim this was one of the greatest achievements in automotive history.

While the factories were retrofitted, the Ford engineers were test driving prototypes of the new Model A. One day a couple of the engineers took the auto out on a test drive and while passing another car, had a head-on collision, throwing the Model A into the ditch, and blasting one of the engineers through the windshield. When Henry and his son, Edsel, inspected the wrecked vehicle, they knew for sure that, even though it was more expensive, the Model A windshield would have laminated (safety) glass. This was a change in the automobile industry that probably saved thousands of lives over the years.

In another test drive, Ford was shaken badly as he attempted to drive over a rough field. He got out of the car and wrote, "Rides too hard. Put on hydraulic shock absorbers." Ford demanded the car be equipped with the Houdaille shock absorbers—the best and most expensive in the world. This feature became the key factor in providing for passenger comfort. Another key addition was using stainless steel for the "bright parts," a costlier but more attractive look. Ford's philosophy on the new car was to use the best, most expensive materials, but make up for the cost through production efficiencies, so the average American could still afford the car.

Ford had something specific in mind for marketing the new vehicle. He asked one of his engineers to take his family on a weekend trip on the experimental Model A. Ford told him: "We ought to see what womenfolk think about it." Ford was quite the Renaissance Man. Not only had he invented and proved the righteousness of the mass production assembly line and masterminded several vehicle improvements, but he had a penchant for brilliant marketing and showmanship. Ford was famous for his Model T promotions with stunts like having the Model

T climb up the stairs of the Tennessee State Capitol and chug to the top of Pikes Peak in Colorado. Stunts the heavier and more expensive cars could not accomplish.

From May 26 into early December 1927, an eager world waited, wondered, and speculated about what the new Ford would look like. *The New York Times*, on Sunday, June 26, featured a lengthy article, "Ford's New Car Keeps the Motor World Guessing," which highlighted the demise of the Motel T and outlined the dubious prospects for the new car. *Reader's Digest*, in its August 1927 issue, joined in the speculation stating, "The new Ford will be either an ineffective gesture or the beginning of a new era in automobile manufacturing." *Time* magazine reported that Edsel Ford claimed, "The [new] car runs 110 miles in two hours and [has a] top speed of 65 mph."

The New York Times credited the changeover as "probably the biggest replacement of plants in the history of American industry." One and one-half million square feet were added for the new car and its 5,580 parts, which required moving, eliminating, changing, or re-placing more than 40,000 machines. Ford brought back thousands of workers who had been laid off when Model T production ended, and trained a total of 200,000 workmen. There were over sixty miles of conveyors that gradually and efficiently moved the flow of parts from machine to machine and department to department. A radical advance allowed the car bodies to be handled by conveyors, hoists, elevators, and transfer tables rather than hauled by trucks and trains. This equipment eliminated the loading, unloading, switching, and moving of 2,500 freight cars a year.

In October 1927, *Ford News* said the final assembly line had been transferred to the River Rouge complex and was now ready for assembly operations. There were 125,000 down payments for the new car. On October 20th, the first Model A engine rolled off the assembly line, and Henry Ford stamped the car "#1" with a hand stamp and machine hammer. Although there is some controversy about who received the first Model A Ford, the Model A museum in Barry County, Michigan assured us in our 2021 visit, that the first Model A was given to Henry Ford's vagabond friend, Thomas Edison.

In late November 1927, Ford started shipping cars, zipped in canvas bags, to showrooms around the world. Other cars were driven to showrooms around the country. A series of five full page ads produced by N.W. Ayer & Son at a cost of $1.3 million, were carried in 2,000 daily newspapers. From 1927 to 1931 Ford spent over $5.2 million on magazine advertising for the new car. Although the Model T was mostly black, the new Model A came in a rainbow of colors including Niagara Blue, Arabian Sand, Dawn Gray, and Gun Metal Blue. The paint finish was a harder and longer lasting pyroxylin lacquer. Standard equipment included a starter, five steel-spoke wheels, windshield wiper, speedometer, gas gauge, ammeter (measures electric current), dash light, mirror, rear and stop lights, oil measuring rod (dipstick), ignition lock, a complete tool set encased in a box on the front fender, and shatterproof glass in the windshield.

In the beginning, there were only five styles: A five passenger Phaeton for $395, the Roadster for $385 or $420 with a rumble seat, the Coupe for $495 or $530 with a rumble seat, the Tudor for $495, and a Sport Coupe with landau irons and rumble seat for $550. Other models were added later.

On December 2, 1927, only one year from the conception of the idea, all the Ford showrooms had a brand-new Model A, with long lines of people waiting to see the new motor car. The eagerly awaited vehicle was received with tremendous enthusiasm throughout the US, Canada, and foreign countries, despite the bad winter weather. *Ford News* magazine claimed over 10.5 million people, or nearly 10 percent of the US population, saw the new car in the first few days. All the cars arrived on time and showed remarkable performance in traveling over snow-drifted roads to get to their showrooms. Within two weeks, about 400,000 orders were placed. *Ford News* said one Model A drove from Dearborn, Michigan to Los Angeles, at high speed in only 90 hours—a distance of about 3,000 miles.

The New York Evening Post on Dec. 3, 1927, reported:

> The new Ford is shown off to a generation which has
> lost the joy of getting its hands dirty. The old Ford
> ruined 10 million pairs of overalls. The new Ford is
> unveiled in hotel ballrooms by salesmen in dinner
> jackets. It has theft-proof coincidental locks, pressure
> grease-gun lubrication, and five steel-spoke wheels.
> [In perfect conditions the automobile] will go 65
> mph and get 30 miles to the gallon. It was made with
> Johansson precision gauges, accurate to the fraction of
> an inch, and wipes its own windshield. It is masculine
> in reliability and feminine in grace.

The New Republic magazine summarized the attributes of the new car:

> It makes every concession to taste and convenience
> which is embodied in cars selling for three or four
> times the price. Four choices of color, stream line
> form, high radiator and hood. Illuminated instrument
> board on the dash. Nickeled radiator and headlights,
> four-wheel brakes, standard gearshift, 20-30 mph.

In one of the promotional ads for the new car on Dec. 2, 1927, Ford
revealed the company values:

> We never forget that people who buy Ford cars are the
> people who helped to make this business big. We are
> able to sell at a low price because we have found new
> ways to give greater value without a great increase in
> our own costs.

Ford Motor also aggressively marketed the car for women. They
understood that advertising in women's magazines from 1923 to

1926 had gone up 665 percent. Magazines aimed at women, such as *Cosmopolitan*, *McCalls*, and the *Women's Home Companion*, all proclaimed the Model A as a "splendid car for the busy mother. Smooth riding ease and restful comfort make the new Ford an especially good car for women to drive." Ford sent a letter to all the dealers, reminding them to keep a clean facility because, "Grease impresses a woman more than it does a man; she can detect dust where the average man would never notice. A pleasing arrangement of accessories or parts in the show cases will impress her very much more than it will her husband. A clean place to stand or sit down is essential. Dirt holds no charms for her."

Ford's advertising program was so effective that in 1927, The Ford Motor Company received the Harvard Advertising Award for a meritorious "national campaign conspicuous in excellence of planning and execution." In 1929, the Model A propelled Ford to capture 37 percent market share and achieve record profits of over $91 million. Production rose to 1,851,092 cars with profitability of $49 per car. Three years later, in 1932, the *Automobile Trade Journal* said Ford's profit per car was still about $42. Ford not only was great at promotions, electronics, and manufacturing, but also finance. Edsel Ford worked with the Guardian Detroit Bank and the Universal Credit company to offer financing for dealers and customers.

Grandpa was paying attention to the Ford Model A promotions and he liked what he read. The new Model A was safe, inexpensive, roomy, and could chug up mountains faster and better than the other cars on the market. In late 1929, despite the ongoing depression around the country, he contacted the local Ford dealer and ordered a black Model A Standard Fordor with a built-in trunk on the back. The Standard Fordor had three windows on each side like the Town Sedan, but the exterior finishes and interior trim were less expensive and luxurious. The interior had piped seats in brown-checked cloth. The seatbacks, quarters, door panels, window curtains, and header were trimmed in plain brown cloth.

The front floor had a black rubber mat, and the rear floor was covered with a brown carpet. The toolbox embedded in the front fender had an adjustable wrench, two open-end wrenches, pliers, screwdriver, combination spark plug and head bolt wrench, instruction book, two tire irons, a jack, grease gun, and tire pump. There was also a lamp bulb kit, tire patch kit, and a tire pressure gauge contained in a snap pouch. Grandpa ordered a custom trunk on the back, which was constructed of basswood, had an extruded metal lip with a rubber gasket to provide a weather-tight seal, and two cowhide straps for security. An extender allowed the trunk to fit between the back of the car and the spare tire. The accessory rack on the running board held three cans to store oil, water, and gasoline. This was a car ready for a long road-trip.

CHAPTER FIVE

1930: THE TRIP BEGINS: CRYSTAL LAKE TO CODY, WYOMING

IT WAS THE SPRING OF 1930 AND AL STENSETH AT THE FORD DEALERSHIP IN FOREST CITY WAS DRIV- ING GRANDPA AND THIRTEEN-YEAR-OLD KEITH TO DES MOINES TO PICK UP THEIR BRAND NEW 1930 MODEL A STANDARD FORDOR. Normally the Ford would have been picked up at the local dealer, but Grandpa wanted the Des Moines Ford assembly plant to install a trunk on the back of the car, which would have brought the price of the car up to about $800. It was thrilling for them to pick up the brand-new car and drive it 132 miles back to Forest City.

Gladys Siekmeier, Grandpa's oldest daughter, remembered that "when they were preparing to leave, Mother worked night and day to get everything ready. Ole [Gladys's husband] and I did not think too much about it, but many people in the neighborhood were envious of them. It was the beginning of the depression, and people wondered how they could afford such a trip." Grandpa and Ole built and installed cupboards on the right-hand side of the car that held the pressure cooker and other kitchen items. The cooker held the enamel plates, cups, and silverware. The factory-made trunk on the back of the car held the tent, beds, and clothes. The factory toolbox was built into the front fender and held the tire irons, tools, and car manuals. They did not quite know how they were going to get everything in the car, but they managed. Grandpa tuned up the car before they left and worried about how they could get the loaded-up car with nine people, to chug up the massive mountains common in the West.

Nearly everything was ready for the big trip. Grandma had spent the year sewing little dresses for one-year-old Marilee, shirts for the older kids, and coats and pajamas for everyone. Since the farmhouse only had electricity for lighting, she used her Singer sewing machine operated by a manual foot pedal called a treadle. Grandpa and all the kids would wear overalls or khaki-colored dark jeans, shirts, and sturdy shoes. Grandma took along a few cotton dresses for herself. Everything was carefully calibrated for the 15-month trip. She had calculated how much the kids would grow and how many clothes could be handed down to each child. Grandma said, "It was not an easy job to always have clean diapers for Marilee, but I managed, and she never had a sore bottom." In the 1920s, one could buy "absorbent white cotton Birdseye hemmed diapers" in the Sears catalog; however, we are quite sure grandma probably made the diapers herself, out of scraps of absorbent cloth.

My grandparents had put together a trip plan and knew exactly how many miles there were between each city and where they could spend the nights. However, they also kept their plans flexible to adjust to the quality of the campsites and the roads.

Before heading out on the big trip, they decided to do a dry run to see if everything worked well. They loaded up the car and traveled a few miles south to spend a few days with relatives in Webster City and Stanhope, and then drove back to Crystal Lake to spend a few days with Gladys and Ole.

After leaving Crystal Lake, they drove 65 miles west to Ayrshire, Iowa, to visit Grandpa's brothers, Omro, Jacob, and their families. During their visit, they drove over to Emmetsburg's Riviera movie theater to watch their first talking movie. The dry run proved a success and they were ready to take on the big adventure. They loaded up the car again and drove straight north to catch old highways 16 and 14, which headed directly west to the Black Hills.

Grandma didn't seem to be concerned about how to entertain seven kids crammed in a car for 15,000 miles. But back then, kids entertained themselves by reading books or playing games. They played games like counting state license plates, different animals seen, and reading Burma Shave signs. The signs were placed strategically along the road to read one by one as you sped by. For example, one series of signs read, "Train approaching/Whistle blowing/Stop/Avoid that run-down feeling/Burma-Shave."

Grandma remembered, "We carried our money in traveler's checks. We lived well as far as food was concerned. Campgrounds were inexpensive and in some state parks the entrance fee took care of the camping spot. Gas costs were high in some places. The roads were not very good, mostly dirt and gravel and there were lots of detours. There were very few tourist homes and they were very expensive, so we camped." Because the roads were rough, it might have taken two or three days to get to the Black Hills—a distance of 561 miles from Crystal Lake.

The first night of camping was probably around Mitchell, South Dakota, the home of the world's only remaining corn palace. The original palace was built in 1892 on the city's main street as a tourist attraction as well as a gathering place for celebrating the fall harvest festival. The exterior and interior murals of the 1930 corn palace displayed scenes of South Dakota life, built from about 275,000 ears of corn. The exterior murals are replaced annually and the interior murals are changed every fifteen to twenty years. The murals are made of dried corn on the cob with eleven different colors, ranging from light tan to a dark reddish black.

The palace is an imposing three-story Moorish building with a number of colorful cone-shaped towers—minarets with American flags flowing on top. According to *The Dakota Farmer*, at least thirty-four corn palaces were built in twenty-four towns across the Midwest between 1880 and 1930. The Mitchell palace is the only one that still remains. The current palace was built in 1930, just in time for the annual Corn Palace Festivities and the first boy's state basketball tournament.

As the family was traveling towards the Black Hills, they passed through the town of Wall, South Dakota, but the famous Wall Drug wasn't built until 1931. Now the drug store is a must-see key attraction on the way to the Black Hills. There are still hundreds of road signs declaring the number of miles to Wall Drug and advertising, in Burma Shave style, what you can buy once you get there. "Get a soda/Get a root beer/Turn next corner/Just as near/To Highway 16 and 14/Free Ice Water/Wall Drug/Only 100 more miles." Passing through Wall, they took a quick detour to the north unit of Badlands National Park and on to Rapid City.

Rapid City has a long and colorful history. In 1804, members of the Lewis and Clark expedition discovered a dinosaur's 45-foot-long articulated vertebral column along the banks of the Missouri River near the city. Since then many other archeological discoveries have been found. Because of these finds, the Works Progress Administration (WPA) in the early 1930s started building a dinosaur park in Rapid City. The current park is located on Hangman's Hill, where three horse thieves were hanged in 1877. In 1874, a US Army expedition discovered gold at French Creek near the Black Hills and the word spread rapidly. However, one of the most significant developments in the city's economic history began in the 1890s, when the newly created Black Hills National Forest started to become a tourist destination.

The emerging Mount Rushmore in 1930.
Courtesy of the Amon Carter Museum of American Art

After staying in Rapid City for the night, the family drove south to see the construction progress on the Mount Rushmore National Memorial. The sixty-foot sculptures of the heads of presidents Washington, Jefferson, Lincoln, and Theodore Roosevelt were to be carved into the mountain's granite face. The family looked up at the surface and saw about a dozen men who had rappelled off the cliff and were chipping away at George Washington's emerging face. It was a massive effort that wasn't completed until 1941.

They continued to drive south to Harney Peak (now called Black Elk Peak) where they all got on horses to ride to the top of the 7,241-foot mountain. One historical record recalled the ride up the hill was a "five-hour ride through timber, across fallen trees, past grazing buffalo, crossing streams and gullies without our horses making one false step." General Custer famously attempted to ride his horse to the summit but did not quite make it. But forty years later, my grandparents with seven small children, managed to skillfully ride their horses up to the top. The historic fire lookout tower had not been built yet, but the long ride up the mountain was worth it to experience the expansive sight of the majestic Black Hills National Forest.

There is also some evidence the family drove a few miles south of Harney Peak to visit the Theodore Roosevelt National Park and the astounding Wind Cave National Park, established in 1903 by President Theodore Roosevelt.

The cave is recognized as the densest cave system in the world, the seventh longest cave (154 miles) in the world, and holds 95 percent of all the boxwork formations in the world. The formations are made of thin blades of calcite that project from cave walls and ceilings, forming a honeycomb pattern.

After the adventure in the Black Hills, they backtracked east on Highway 14 and then north on highway 83 to Bismarck and Turtle Lake, North Dakota, to visit Grandpa's cousins. The Lewis and Clark Expedition named this spot Missouri Crossing, because this is where they crossed the Missouri river. In 1873, the Northern Pacific Railway renamed the city Bismarck, in honor of the German Chancellor Otto von Bismarck. It is the only state capital named after a foreign statesman. The railroad had hoped this honorarium would attract Germans to the area, but it was the gold seekers and tourists that eventually flocked to the city. After Bismarck, they drove north to Turtle Lake to visit cousins and explore the nearby Sullys Hill National Park, which was downgraded to a wildlife preserve in 1931.

On the next leg of the trip, the family drove about 400 miles west on old Highway 10 to reach Billings, Montana. If the roads were good, people could travel about 300 miles in a day if they could speed along at 40 or 50 mph. But in all likelihood the roads were rough so the trip would have been slower, the kids would need several stops, and Grandpa didn't like to drive too many miles in one day. On the way they passed through the Little Missouri National Grassland and what is now a large group of national forests. They drove through Miles City and Glendive which followed the jagged route along the Yellowstone River. On the way they stopped at a large rock formation called Pompey's Pillar, which encompasses fifty-one acres on the banks of the Yellowstone River. The family peeled out of the car and started to climb the 200-foot edifice. There are hundreds of markings, petroglyphs, and inscriptions left by visitors, including William Clark from the Lewis and Clark Expedition. Grandpa loved history, and had intensely studied all the national parks and other sites along the route. He loved to regale the kids with stories and the history of each site.

The family had been driving on what seemed like endless strips of Montana roads lined with a sea of cool forests and empty grasslands. However, at last they spotted on the far, far horizon the first dark blue shadows of the white-peaked mountains of the Absaroka Range and the kids squealed with delight.

They arrived in the town of Billings and set up camp. The city was nicknamed the "Magic City" because of its rapid growth after its founding in 1882. It is ringed by massive sandstone bluffs called the Rimrocks and lies in the foothills of the nearby mountain range. It was the first city where the family felt like they were in the real "West." People were dressed in cowboy shirts, jeans, and large cowboy hats. There were covered wagons and people traveled on horses.

The next day they got up early and were eager to drive the 100 miles on old highway 310 to the famous Cody, Wyoming. The kids were very excited to land in a genuine ridin', ropin' cowboy town. They could already see Yellowstone's massive 13,000-foot mountains rising so high in the distance that it seemed like they took up the entire sky.

Aunt Pauline wrote, "When we got to the West, I remember we could see the mountains but it took so long to get to them. We had never seen mountains, and could hardly wait to reach the foothills. I remember the beauty of the mountain streams and how we stopped and Dad let us climb on the rocks in the streams. I sat on a big rock and the sun was so warm, I didn't want to move.

"I remember crossing the Continental Divide. Dad must have studied all about the country, because he knew where everything was.

One day we took a short cut and found ourselves on a mountain road with no guard rails. It seemed about a million feet straight down. We were on the outside and met another car coming up the mountain. All of us had to get out of the car while Dad eased on by with only inches to spare."

Grandma said they spent several nights in Cody because it was a stunningly beautiful place, with a very nice campground. The city is located on the Shoshone River in the Bighorn Basin just fifty miles from the east entrance of Yellowstone National Park. When the Chicago, Burlington, and Quincy Railroad expressed interest in building a line to Cody, the Cody Land Company, eager to have the railroad connection, sold the majority of the town lots to the railroad. When my grandparents rolled through Cody, they likely attended the Cody Stampede, a rodeo and festival the town has held every year since 1919. At that time, the town encouraged all its citizens to dress in cowboy gear to please the tourists. Authentic frontier buildings from the 1890s also inspired people to stop and stay in Cody.

Cody was founded in 1896 by the legendary Colonel William F. "Buffalo Bill" Cody. Cody was born in a log cabin in LeClaire, Iowa, in 1846, the same year that Iowa became a state. He was involved in nearly every key moment of western expansion, including gold prospecting, and stints as a Pony Express rider, army scout, stagecoach driver, buffalo hunter, Civil War soldier, and Indian fighter. However, his love and legacy was his namesake, the town of Cody, where he reportedly spent most of his wealth promoting and building the town.

At one point, the Kansas Pacific branch of the Union Pacific Railroad offered Cody a job of procuring meat for its construction workers. For the next eighteen months, he earned his sobriquet of "Buffalo Bill" by killing more than 4,000 bison. Later, Cody was awarded the Congressional Medal of Honor for gallantry in battles with the US Calvary. The medal was rescinded in 1916, because he was only a civilian scout at the time, not a formal soldier; however, it was restored in 1989.

Cody might have remained a minor frontier figure, but after the Indian Wars and the defeat of Custer at Little Bighorn on June 25, 1876, the wild frontier suddenly became frontpage news all over the world. Shortly after Custer was killed, Cody, traveling with the Fifth Cavalry, encountered Indians near Hat Creek and War Bonnet Creek. Allegedly, Cody managed to avenge Custer's defeat by killing Yellow Hair, a Cheyenne chief, and supposedly scalping him, raising the bloody mass in the air, and declaring, "First Scalp for Custer."

In order to capitalize on his fame and the growing world-wide interest in the "Wild West," Cody created his Wild West show in 1883, which traveled throughout the US and Europe for nearly thirty years. In 1887, Cody's show played for Queen Victoria's Golden Jubilee, marking the fiftieth anniversary of her accession. The show reenacted stagecoach robberies, buffalo-hunting, Pony Express runs, and a melodramatic Custer's Last Stand.

In 1895, circus great James A. Bailey of Barnum and Bailey, joined Cody and revolutionized the show. Rather than traveling from town to town on wagons and horses, Bailey loaded all the equipment, hundreds of horses and buffaloes, and the 500-person staff on two trains with fifty plus cars. In 1899, the Wild West show covered over 11,000 miles in 200 days giving 341 performances in 132 cities in the US. In most places, there would be a parade and a couple of two-hour performances. Sadly, the shows were mostly based on myths, which always put the Native Americans as the hostile aggressors—attacking wagon trains, settler's cabins, and Custer's soldiers. The public evidently needed to embrace a myth that portrayed Native Americans as war-bonneted warriors, and the last impediment to civilization. The show finally came to an end when interest in the wild west shootouts declined and moved on to the contemporary pastimes of movies, radio, baseball, and football.

The winners of wars always get to write history, but sometimes the truth does come out. Historians have found that attacks on settlers' wagons and homes were rarer than reported, and the Indian Wars had a deeper background story. US Treaties had guaranteed the Lakota, Dakota Sioux, and the Arapaho, exclusive possession of the Dakota territory west of the Missouri River. However, after gold was discovered on the land, the US government was unwilling to remove settlers and prospectors and unsuccessful in negotiating with the tribes, so the US forcibly tried to remove the tribes from their land. The tribes reasonably fought back to protect their territory.

Even though Cody made sure the Indians who performed in the show were paid and treated equitably, he might never have imagined the lasting power his myths had on the American psyche. Even General William Tecumseh Sherman called the shows "wonderfully realistic and historically reminiscent." Mark Twain announced that the shows were "genuine down to its smallest details."

Grandma remembered, "After we left Cody, we stopped in the Shoshone National Forest, a wilderness area with rugged mountains covered with pine, fir, and aspens. It was a very interesting place because of its steep canyons, large glaciers, and over 500 lakes. There were supposed to be grizzly bears around, but fortunately, we did not see any." The Shoshone Forest was the first federally protected national forest in the US and covers nearly 2.4 million acres, with its endless, monstrous, snow-capped mountains.

When the family arrived at Chimney Rock at Shoshone, the kids tumbled out of the car and hiked up the towering 315-foot rock formation via the Outcroppings Trail. At the top they soaked in the 75-mile panoramic views of Hickory Nut Gorge and Lake Lure. All this climbing near the end of the day was a clever ruse my grandparents imposed to tire the kids out so they would get to bed early.

Sure enough, after the big climb, the kids were tired and ready to get to Yellowstone, set up camp, and devour their dinner.

CHAPTER SIX

1930: YELLOWSTONE NATIONAL PARK

WHEN ROLLING INTO YELLOWSTONE NATIONAL PARK IN JULY OF 1930, MY FAMILY PROBABLY DIDN'T REALIZE THAT JUST A FEW YEARS BEFORE, THE PARK HAD BEEN SUFFERING FROM AN EXISTENTIAL CRISIS. Most of the country was probably not aware of how close we came to destroying the natural beauty and frangible biosystem of our national parks. In the last half of the nineteenth century, Congress had little interest in developing or protecting our natural treasures, but the powerful and monopolistic railroads understood the opportunity. They greased the congressional machinery and not only got support for a cross-country railroad system, but support for creating the world's first national park in Yellowstone in 1872—a perceived magical playground and hunting arena for the railroads' wealthy customers.

Although Congress voted for the creation of Yellowstone, it did not appropriate any funding to care for or provide any protection for the park. As a result, no one was in charge and the park was being exploited by the railroads, mining companies, tourists, and game hunters. Animals were killed to sell their skins and their carcasses were stripped off and dumped in the snow. Just for fun, tourists and hunters rolled boulders down the canyon walls. Forests were razed, campfires blazed out of control, minerals were mined, plans were in place to lay railroad tracks in the park, and independent tour groups set up shop and charged exorbitant rates. Aristocratic hunters from all over the world, like the British Earl of Dunraven, built their own hunting lodges in the parks, and found it was "cheaper and more adventurous to be in the US parks than having a private preserve in Scotland or a house in London."

If there was one group who was trying to establish control of the parks, it was the railroads. This was not surprising because at the last half of the nineteenth century, the railroads had become masters of the universe and Congress was eager to gift them enormous amounts of land in order to develop a railroad system across the Wild West. The railroads sold bonds to the public and used the funds to build the railways and develop the towns around the major stops. The Northern Pacific Railroad advertised their bonds would give bondholders a lien "upon millions of acres of the finest land in the country." The bonds were "secured by a first and only mortgage on over 2,000 miles of railroad tracks, and over 23,000 acres of land for every mile of finished road." Who wouldn't buy those bonds?

It took more than bonds to develop this massive transportation system across America. The railroads needed paying passengers and destination spots for wealthy tourists, so they immediately built huge, luxury, full-service destination hotels all over Canada and the US. Their target audience was all the Gilded Age robber barons and their families. These successful, monopolistic industrialists had built ships, cars, banks, steel factories, and now their families were ready to party. Their typical party venues were all over the world—Europe,

Africa, Asia—any place exotic and entertaining. To lure people to stay in America, the railroads invented a "See America First" campaign, to entice the wealthy to blow off the rest of world, get on a train, and see the wondrous sights and hunt the exotic animals right here in America. It worked! Wealthy tourists and game hunters from all over the world signed on in droves.

Originally, the railroads built over one hundred of these luxury tourist hotels and some are still around today: The Grand Hotel on Mackinac Island, Michigan, The Del Coronado in San Diego, The Sagamore Resort and the Mohonk Mountain House in New York, the Mount Washington Resort in Bretton Woods, New Hampshire, the Fairmont Chateau at Lake Louise and the Fairmont Banff Springs Resort, both in Canada, Old Faithful Inn in Yellowstone, and El Tovar at the Grand Canyon.

By the end of the nineteenth century, wealthy tourists and hunters from all over the world flocked to Yellowstone to see the geysers, mountains, sulfur springs, and giant waterfalls in the most geologically active place in the world. Many came to hunt the wild animals and soon the buffaloes and other animals were nearly wiped out.

Railroad and mining interests continued to lobby Congress to pass bills that would have allowed railroads, mining companies, and others to build facilities through, in, and around the park. It is somewhat of a miracle that Yellowstone was not seriously damaged by the iron horses and the mining interests. In the late nineteenth century, there were 237 mining companies excavating in the park and they desperately wanted the railroads to build tracks through the park so they could save on transportation costs. The mining companies were paying $25 a ton to move the minerals by horse-drawn wagon, but having railroad tracks spread around Yellowstone would have brought the cost down to $5 a ton.

Of greater concern to many, was the high price on buffalo heads that encouraged their slaughter and threatened the cumbersome creatures with extinction. In 1800, there were an estimated 60 million American bison in this country. By the end of the century, there were only a few hundred of these massive creatures left. It has been called the worst animal genocide in the history of the world, but fortunately, the greatest recovery from the brink of extinction, as there are now over 400,000 bison in this country. But they weren't the only species to be hunted and trapped. In 1891, the Zoological Park in Washington, D.C., supervised by the Smithsonian, was busy in Yellowstone trapping moose, buffalo, antelope, black and grizzly bears, foxes, porcupines, mountain sheep, mountain lions, wolverines, wildcats, mink, badgers, beavers, and others for shipment to the national zoo.

So, at the end of the nineteenth century, the mining companies, hunters, railroads, and even the national zoo had a shared interest in keeping control of the park for their own personal use. Fortunately, in the 1870s, painter Thomas Moran and photographer William Henry Jackson, joined the Hayden Expedition to explore and document Yellowstone and find the best routes to build railroads from the Mississippi to the Pacific Coast. In a twist of luck, Moran's paintings and Jackson's photographs eventually captured the imagination of the public and Congress, and inspired a conservation movement throughout the country. Finally, the Lacey Act of 1900, promoted by Iowa congressman John F. Lacey and Theodore Roosevelt, was enacted and the animals and the land were saved from extinction. But it wouldn't be until 1916, when President Woodrow Wilson signed the National Park Service Act, that the parks were fully protected from the hunters, railroads, mining companies, and poachers. Up until 1916, the railroads could still pretty much build and do what they wanted to in the parks. By 1903, the Northern Pacific Railroad had already built the Old Faithful Inn just a few feet from the Old Faithful geyser and the Yellowstone Lake Hotel next to Yellowstone Lake.

At first the secretary of the interior prohibited motor cars from entering the park, with the reasoning that backfires from cars would terrify the animals. But there were many forces promoting the use of cars in the national parks. At the time, only the very wealthy could afford the trip to Yellowstone, which included a long railroad ride to the north entrance, and then a five-day-long stagecoach ride to Yellowstone. However, many people wanted to democratize the national parks, and the best way to do that was to allow the average family to drive their motor cars into the parks. The well-organized motor car clubs were aggressively lobbying Congress and the public, as were the General Federation of Women's Clubs who boasted over 2 million loyal and active members.

All these citizen movements came to a deafening crescendo a couple of years before the 1915 Panama-Pacific Exposition. Many people expected thousands of tourists would want to drive through Yellowstone on their way to the Expos. On July 31, 1915, the government finally allowed the first motor car to roll into the north entrance. It was a Model T Runabout, the first "tin can tourist" in Yellowstone. As a result of the new policy, the park had a record 51,895 visitors in 1915. Word caught on fast, because in 1930, when my grandparents visited, there were 227,901 visitors to the park that year. When we visited Yellowstone in 2021 with our grandson, there were 3.4 million visitors, even though the country was in the middle of the Covid-19 pandemic.

Only fifteen years after the first "tin can tourist" entered Yellowstone, my grandparents chugged into the east entrance. The kids had a list of things they wanted to see: Old Faithful, giant waterfalls, buffaloes and bears, geysers, mud pots, and hot springs. The park has a paved 142-mile Grand Loop Road that makes a giant figure eight in the center of the park. All five entrances lead to the Loop. Grandpa had spent many hours poring over the information on the park and had a plan. When they drove from Cody into the east entrance, they would be near the bottom of the "figure eight." They would start there and proceed up the west side of the loop to catch Old Faithful and many of the geysers and mud pots. Then they would drive east through the middle of the "figure eight" and up and down the east side to catch the Upper and Lower Falls, and the lookout on Mount Washburn. Then they would drive to the top of the loop, see Mammoth Springs, and proceed out the north entrance to Montana. At some point in the trip they

ventured south of the Loop and made a quick visit to the spectacular
Grand Tetons, which had just become a national park in 1929.

As soon as they reached Yellowstone Lake and the entrance to the
Grand Loop, they paid the $6 entrance and camping fee, and quickly
set up camp and gobbled up their dinner. They were exhausted from
the day's hiking and adventure, fell fast asleep, and didn't notice the
quiet snowflakes falling from the dark sky. They woke up to a winter
wonderland with several inches of new snow piled on the tent and the
car. These Iowa kids knew exactly how to deal with a few inches of
snow. They put on every piece of clothing they owned and immediately
started snowball fights and made snow angels. Grandpa got up early
and started the campfire and Grandma made oatmeal.

After breakfast they were on their way to Old Faithful following
the road around Yellowstone Lake and crossing the continental divide.
They stopped for a while at West Thumb and watched people feed the
bears. As they continued to cruise down the highway, the kids were
watching an open field looking for animals. Suddenly, Keith yelled out,
"Dad, there is a grizzly bear chasing a buffalo and they are going faster
than we are." Richard chimed in, "Faster Dad, let's beat those animals."
Both animals were running fast for a purpose: the grizzly bear was
hungry and the buffalo did not want to be his lunch. The car was cruis-
ing along about 35 mph so the kids were shocked the two mammoth
creatures could run that fast.

Suddenly, they noticed an area of dense trees ahead of the animals.
What would happen? The buffalo quickly realized he would be caught if
he charged into the woods, so he took a sharp left and ran right in front
of their Model A and kept marching in front of it. The buffalo slowed
down because he knew he was saved, but the kids were terrified. The
buffalo seemed bigger and more massive than their car. The American
bison can weigh over 2,000 pounds and stands up to 6 feet tall. Would
the buffalo charge their car? Were they safe? Grandpa explained to the
kids that Yellowstone is the only place in the US where bison have con-
tinuously lived since prehistoric times. Bison can spin around quickly,

jump high fences, swim fast, and run up to 40 mph. Both the male and female have horns. They usually travel in herds, but this one was all alone. Grandpa slowed down and advised the kids to look at the bison's tail. If it stood straight up, it could be ready to charge and they would have to quickly make their escape. The kids quietly held their breath, but soon the bison wandered off the road, without even acknowledging the Model A, creeping slowly behind it.

The family saw hundreds of bears, bison, deer, elk, and other animals in the park, but they did not spot a single wolf, because the last wolf pack in Yellowstone was killed off in 1926. In fact, by the mid-1920s, wolves had been almost entirely eliminated from all forty-eight states. Many people felt wolves should be eliminated because they were a threat to ranchers and their animals. However, others felt the animals in the parks were getting too fat and lazy, without a natural predator to chase them. It wasn't until 1995, that Interior Secretary Bruce Babbitt, imported thirty-one gray wolves from Canada and released the beasts into Yellowstone. He later remarked that releasing the foreign wolves "electrified" the entire animal ecosystem in the park.

When they finally reached Old Faithful, the kids were relieved and piled out of the car. Yellowstone is centered on top of the Yellowstone Caldera, the largest super volcano on the continent, measuring 1,350 square miles. It is considered an active volcano and the hotspot has created more than 10,000 geothermal features, including 300 geysers. There are four types of geothermal features in the park: geysers and hot springs, which contain substantial water; and fumaroles and mud pots, which contain a limited amount of water.

The kids looked around and felt like they had landed on a far-away planet. The ground looked gray, barren, and void of vegetation. The air was saturated with the smell of sulfur, the ground was bubbling with ponds holding bright blue scalding water, and a giant geyser was spouting water nearly 200 feet in the air. It seemed like a biblical place for moral and spiritual rejuvenation. The scalding mud pots seemed like a

1930 postcard of the interior of Old Faithful Inn

gateway to hell, but the giant geyser, open sky, and massive mountains seemed like a stairway to heaven.

Within a few feet of the Old Faithful geyser, stood one of the largest, most interesting buildings the kids had ever seen. The giant, steeply sloped log hotel rose in the air as high as the Old Faithful geyser and sported a number of colorful flags on the roof. The huge bright-red 2-inch thick, double-planked front doors, were strapped in heavy wrought iron and bejeweled with more than a hundred iron studs. The seven-foot-high doors, each with a peephole grill, were supported by heavy iron hinges and fitted with a twenty-five-pound iron lock and key, which gave it the feel of a medieval castle.

As they walked into the hotel, they were astonished to see the huge lobby extending several stories to the roof, with balconies surrounding each floor of the hotel. The interior ceiling was made of giant logs closely fitted together. The lobby's focal point was a giant fireplace made from 500 tons of locally quarried rhyolite stone, encasing four large hearths. The smell of fresh popcorn filled the lobby. At the end of the lobby, the adjoining space boasted a massive, half-octagon-shaped dining room 62 feet across with large plate glass windows so diners could watch Old Faithful spout while they leisurely ate their meals.

Grandma encouraged the kids to run up the hundred steps to the top and look down on the lobby from the top floor and then run up to the "Widow's Walk" on the roof. She also made it known they could have the popcorn, but they could not eat in the restaurant because it was too expensive. She told them there were delicious peanut butter and sliced banana sandwiches in the car that they could devour on the outdoor picnic tables. Much more fun.

That night the family camped near the Old Faithful Inn. It was so dark you could see every star in the sky. There was a giant US Navy searchlight on the hotel roof to illuminate nighttime viewing of Old Faithful, so the kids stayed up half the night watching the hourly eruptions. After the young kids were put safely in bed and the older kids ready to baby-sit, Grandma and Grandpa dashed over to the Old Faithful Inn and danced to the music of the Fred Gebert Orchestra, playing from the elevated balcony. The orchestra did their gig six days a week from 1928 to 1932. The family discovered that staying up late dancing and watching Old Faithful proved to be much more fun than milking cows and slopping pigs at 6 a.m. before school. Memories of the tedious, hard farm life were beginning to fade as the family immersed themselves in this fantasy land.

Grandma remembered: "At 7 p.m., the forest rangers would build a big fire. They took long logs and set them up in wigwam fashion. The flames would leap way up into the air. The rangers would talk about the main features of the park and the life of the bears, roast marshmallows, and then we would all sing. After singing, we attended a movie picture of Yellowstone given at the museum. The people were very friendly."

Eleven-year-old Pauline wrote that she was most impressed with the rangers. "We stayed there about a week. It was the most beautiful place to me. I wore khaki pants that came just below my knees and a shirt. I had straight hair with bangs hanging in my eyes. I fell in love with the rangers in the park and the stories they told. I still have

Lower Falls on the Yellowstone River

pictures in my mind of the falls, the mountains, the mud pots and, of course, Old Faithful."

After leaving Old Faithful, the family stopped at Lower, Midway, and Upper Geyser Basins. The Upper Geyser basin contains Old Faithful. The Midway Geyser is small in size, but its geothermal features are large and colorful. The Lower Geyser has all four types of geothermal features, but one of the highlights are the Fountain Paint Pots, which look like giant bubbling cauldrons. After driving through the Norris Geyser Basin, the family turned east and camped in the Canyon Village. Just a little bit south of Canyon Village are the phenomenal Upper and Lower Falls. They are at the southern tip of the Grand Canyon of Yellowstone which runs twenty miles upriver to the Tower Falls. The canyon was formed by erosion as the Yellowstone River flowed over progressively softer, less resistant rock. The 100-foot Upper Falls and the 300-foot Lower Falls can be seen from a number of trails and viewpoints. The entire family made the arduous walks up and down the trails to see all the vantage points of the falls. They were quite ready for bed after those long and spectacular walks.

The next adventure was driving to the top of Mount Washburn, which has an elevation of 10,219 feet. The grade to Mount Washburn is not too steep for the average motor car, but one must be careful. The road hugs the cliff above a sheer drop of a thousand feet. Sudden sharp turns make you feel suspended between the sky and the bottom of the canyon. However, the adventure is worth it, because when you arrive at the top, there are spectacular views for a hundred miles in each direction.

The last major stop in the park was Mammoth Hot Springs, which has been described as an inside-out cave. The rain and melted snow during the year seep deep down underground and are heated from a partially molten magma chamber. The hot water rises and mixes with hot gases and carbon dioxide, which dissolves the limestone on its way to the surface and then dribbles down the sides. Liberty Cap is one of the best-known features and rises as high as a four-story building.

As they were driving out of the north entrance of the park on their way to Montana, the family was somewhat melancholy. Yellowstone was an unbelievable, magical place they could never possibly have imagined. They thought they would never see anything as majestic ever again in their lifetimes.

Grandma wrote:

> Every kid had a job. We always left our camping space as clean as we found it, many times more so. We were complimented several times on how well our gang behaved. My job was cooking. We had a hot breakfast, then stopped at noon and had a cold lunch. At night, we usually had a good, hot meal. There were lots of bears in the park, and they were always looking for food at night. We had to make sure we did not leave any food out.
>
> At most [camp sites] there were showers, running water, toilets, and usually washing machines and irons were available. In those days we did not have the good fabrics that didn't need ironing. When we found a good camp site, we usually stopped for several days to do laundry and rest. There were swings and other playground equipment at the campsites, and the kids loved to play baseball. The kids were very cooperative and everyone had a job, so it took very little time to set up camp. We bought food in grocery stores and fruit and vegetable stands. Mostly, we bought bread, meat, eggs, milk, vegetables, fruit, and breakfast food.

Pauline remembered, "Dad and Keith put up the tent, and we all helped put up the beds, while Mom did the cooking in the pressure cooker on the gas stove. We were all glad to get out and run around the camps. There were always other people around, and Dad was a very friendly person. I really enjoyed the trip, but sometimes I got tired of riding even though we did not drive very far in a day. We stopped at every place that was of any interest. Sometimes we would spend several days at one place."

Leaving Yellowstone was sad for the family because they couldn't imagine they would ever find another place so intriguing, vast, and exciting. But they had high hopes, and they were on their way to Montana to visit more cousins. Grandpa had a lot of cousins who had settled all over the country for a very simple reason. In the era of primogeniture in Iowa farming, when the parents retired or passed away, the eldest son typically would inherit the entire farming operation. This meant the daughters needed to either get married or support themselves as a nurse or teacher. If they didn't marry, they were called spinsters and typically lived with relatives. The younger sons had to go off and find another occupation or buy another farm either in Iowa or in other states. Levi Sr. had seven children, but only one son could inherit the farm. Levi Sr.'s seven children had a couple of dozen kids of their own and only a few of them were on the list to inherit the same family farms. As a result, many of Grandpa's cousins were farmers scattered around Iowa, North Dakota, Montana, Idaho, Washington, Oregon, California, and Colorado. Grandpa scheduled the entire trip around visiting all his cousins and the national parks along the way. Grandma only had one aunt in Oklahoma to visit.

CHAPTER SEVEN

1930: ON THE WAY TO THE WEST COAST

CALIFORNIA HERE WE COME! Only a couple thousand more miles. Grandma recalled, "The first night out of Yellowstone, we camped at Bozeman, Montana. We crossed the Continental Divide at Deer Lodge Pass, elevation 5,815 feet, then went on to Idaho. Usually there were lots of people traveling and stopping at auto camps and everyone was eager to talk. At that time, the most popular question was, 'Well, how many miles did you drive today?'. There were plenty of gas stations, but some were 50 miles or more apart and prices varied wildly." During this leg of the trip, the family spent several days with relatives in Montana and Idaho.

Grandma remembered, "Many people had trouble with overheated motors on mountain roads, but our Ford never caused any trouble. We drove it several years after we were back home, and years later Pauline and Richard drove it to high school in Forest City. We finally traded it in on a new car. On the way to deliver it to the dealer, it collapsed on the edge of Forest City. It had been a very good, reliable Ford."

The family drove northwest on old highway 10 through Butte, Missoula, Coeur d'Alene, and Spokane, to Wenatchee, Washington to visit the apple orchard owned by Grandpa and his cousin, Lee Spaulding. Wenatchee, the "apple capital of the world," is snuggled at the base of snow-covered Cascade mountains and rests at the confluence of the Columbia and Wenatchee Rivers. In 1893, the Great Northern Railway completed its St. Paul to Seattle line straight through Wenatchee, finally allowing freight shipments of wheat, apples, and other products to markets around the country.

Grandma wrote, "Lee Spaulding shipped several carloads of apples to Iowa each year until the government legislated so many regulations that he sold the orchard." .

They camped for a few days with the Spaulding family and also with Grandpa's Aunt Mary. Mary's sister, Aunt Fanny, was a very good cook and served them a bear roast for dinner, which the family thought was delicious.

Grandma remembered, "The people around that area had small orchards and many of them grew Bing cherries. One day we were driving around and stopped at a Bing cherry orchard. Levi asked the owner how much he would charge to let us eat as many as we wanted. The owner said it would cost a dollar, including a basketful we could take with us." The Bing cherry is a delicious, sweet, dark purple berry that was originally cultivated in Oregon by a horticulturist and his Manchurian Chinese foreman, Ah Bing, for whom the cultivar was named.

The next leg of the trip from Wenatchee was through the Okanogan-Wenatchee National Forest and the North Cascades National Park, straight north to Bellingham, to visit Grandpa's aunt and cousins. Bellingham sits near the gigantic Mount Baker in what is now the North Cascades National Park, only about 20 miles from the Canadian border. The family decided to drive up a few miles in Canada to stay in a camp

Grandpa (left) with his cousin, Lee Spaulding

near a large lake. In those days, passports existed, but American citizens didn't need one to go back and forth to Canada or Mexico.

Leaving Canada, they took the relatively short drive to Seattle, which turned out to be not only the first industrial city they had ever seen, but also the first time they had a close-up view of the Pacific Ocean. Of course, a true Seattleite knows it is really the Puget Sound, which is a smaller body of salt water connected to an ocean. In 1930, Seattle was a town of contradictions. In the first couple of decades in the twentieth century, Seattle had secured itself as a sophisticated city. The thriving timber and maritime industries had created a city eager to provide its citizens all the artistic and architectural thrills of an east coast metropolis.

Between 1905 and 1912, the city had hired the famous landscape architects, the Olmsted Brothers, to design and construct a number of connecting city parks and boulevards that added a sense of majesty to the city. In 1914, the 38-story Smith Tower was completed and became the tallest building west of the Mississippi. That same year, the city completed the leveling of Denny Hill to allow for further downtown development. The Seattle Art Museum, the Seattle Symphony, the Cornish Art School, and the majestic Olympic Hotel were all built in this era. The Pike Place farmer's market was a draw for locals and tourists. An effective city-wide trolley car system, a series of impressive bridges, and the Lake Washington Ship Canal and locks vastly improved the transportation system.

However, behind this colonial economy, was a broiling labor movement that continually questioned the social order and challenged the hegemony of the local captains of industry. In 1913, the Seattle Potlatch Riot broke out when throngs of tourists, sailors, and locals turned the streets into a full-scale brawl, destroying anything related to the socialist cause. There was a deep division in the community over the competing philosophies of patriotism, socialism, and the rights of workers to express their concerns.

In 1919, the first general strike in the nation's history began in Seattle, when 35,000 shipyard workers, who had agreed to wage freezes during WWI, failed to receive their promised war-end increases and declared a strike. The Seattle Central Labor Council, representing 110 local unions sympathetic to the cause, joined the effort, and a total of 65,000 workers laid down their tools and marched en masse on the streets. This strike emboldened dozens of unions across the country to also go on strike.

After the stock market crash of 1929, many of the Seattleites continued to question whether capitalism was really working. With the crash of the economy, high unemployment, and homelessness, some of the political leaders in Seattle were embracing the theories of socialism and communism, thinking there must be a better system. It's a zeitgeist in Seattle that has lasted for more than a century.

When my family entered downtown Seattle, they were thrilled to see the tall buildings, gigantic shipping yards, Pike Place Market, and world class mountain and Puget Sound views. They were hoping to stay at the Seattle autocamp, the third largest in the country, developed at the northern end of Woodland Park, overlooking Green Lake. However, the camp was closed in 1928 due to problems in policing and maintenance. As the family continued to drive south, they looked up to the sky on a bright blue August day and were stunned to see Mount Rainier in the distance. The gigantic snow-capped mountain dominated the sky and seemed to be floating, suspended in mid-air. But when they looked down they were saddened to see the new beginnings of Seattle's "Hooverville" camp of homeless men in shanties and shacks.

Early 1930s Seattle Hooverville. Courtesy of the Seattle Municipal Archives #191876

Nearly a year after the great stock market crash, this sight became the first evidence they saw of the frightening poverty, homelessness, and unemployment caused by the over-exuberance of Wall Street.

Their next stop was Mount Rainier National Park, established in 1899, which contains an active volcano, and the most glaciated peak in the contiguous US, spawning nine major rivers draining down the mountain. John Muir, the photographer of many national parks in the late nineteenth century, called the park, "The most luxuriant and the most extravagantly beautiful of all the alpine gardens I ever beheld in all my mountain-top wanderings." Although Muir did not consider himself a mountain climber, he was among the group of explorers who completed the mountain's fifth recorded ascent. It was the first ascent documented by photography and Muir's book called *Ascent of Mount Rainier*. Each year, thousands of people attempt to climb the final three miles from Camp Muir, to reach the peak of Mount Rainier, but less than half succeed.

The family drove as far as they could up the roads in the park and hiked a number of trails. Grandma mentioned, "We had no trouble with the car [at Rainier], but many cars could not make it up the hill. There was a good campground and a beautiful lake in the area." They camped near the Paradise Inn, which opened in 1917 and held a dining room lit by Japanese lanterns and seating up to 400 people. The Inn was one of the few large hotels in national parks that weren't built by the railroads. Instead it was built by the Rainier National Park Company, formed by a group of Tacoma businessmen.

After leaving Rainier, they traveled about forty miles to Puyallup. Grandma wrote , "While we were in Puyallup, we visited the statue of Ezra Meeker, who was one of the town's most celebrated citizens. He came to Washington by prairie schooner in 1852, prospered as a hops farmer, and became well known for his writings on agricultural subjects and his books on pioneers." Grandpa was vitally interested in Meeker, because the Cottington family had a long history of growing hops.

My great-great-great-grandpa, Robert Cottington, was born early in the nineteenth century, near Kent, in the county of Sussex, England.

Kent is known as the "Garden of England" and its center of hop growing. It is surmised that hops were first introduced to England by the
Roman soldiers. Robert farmed the hop gardens and had thirteen children, one of whom was my great-great-grandpa Jesse.

In 1841, when Jesse was about twenty-five years old, he wanted to
take his wife, Rebecca and their three small sons, my great-grandpa
Levi, and his two older brothers James and Edward, to the great land of
opportunity—America. Of the one million foreign passengers arriving
in the US between 1820 and 1845, 63 percent were from the British
Isles, and they typically booked steerage on one of the large steam ships.
The trip would take about two weeks, but Jesse had what he thought
was a better idea. He acquired a small sailboat and sailed his family to
America, taking six arduous weeks to complete the journey.

Nearly a century later, my great-aunt Faith wrote, "My father, Levi
[Sr.] was only a few months old on the trip [across the ocean], and cried
so much that his father wanted to throw him overboard. However, my
grandma, Rebecca, saved the day when she told Jesse, "Let's keep him,
he might amount to something." Rebecca was right. Levi (Sr.) turned
out to be a decorated Civil War hero, a prosperous farmer, a father of
seven, and a successful community leader.

After a six-week journey across the wide, deep, lumpy ocean, my
great-great-grandpa Jesse finally arrived in the port of New York, ready
for opportunity in America. He soon found employment for seven years
in Waterville, New York, cultivating the hop yards of Palmer Seedling
Company. In his continual search for a farm of his own, Jesse in 1851,
migrated to Westfield, Sauk County, Wisconsin, and soon sent for a
half acre's planting of hop roots from New York.

According to the *History of Reedsburg and the Upper Baraboo Valley*:

> In 1853, [Jesse] Cottington harvested the first hop
> crop in Wisconsin. He built a hopkiln of logs, size
> 12 by 12 feet, minus windows and without a stove to
> heat it. By burning a pit of charcoal in the middle of

the structure, the hops could be dried. The first crop yielded only 150 pounds, but Cottington found the Wisconsin soil was better than either New York or Kent, England, for growing hops. He drove the hops to Columbus, Wisconsin with one horse and a hand-made wagon, and received thirty cents a pound for the crop—45 dollars in gold.

Jesse experienced great difficulty in marketing the hops, but finally found a good market by giving a written guarantee to brewers in Madison and Portage that his hops were equal or better in quality to the New York hops. For the first fifteen years of growing, Jesse made five-year contracts, with an initial price of twenty cents a pound. He also provided hop roots to his neighbors, and according to the *History of Reedsburg*:

> [Cottington] was the reason the crops spread until the great crop of 1867 netted the growers in the area $2 million. It was not uncommon in 1866-67 for a person without capital to buy a farm for $3-4,000, grow four or five acres of hops with a price of 45-60 cents a pound, pay for the entire farm, and have $1,000 left over.

According to Wisconsin's Hop Raising Official Marker:

> Hops were introduced to Wisconsin in 1852 by Jesse Cottington, and hop culture reached its peak in 1866-7 when this area was called the greatest primary hop district in the US.

There is a piece of irony here, because Jesse and his family were notorious teetotalers.

However, great prices don't last forever, and competition and crop disease caused the hop crash of 1868, which bankrupted half the farmers in the area. This disruption was very similar to the dramatic price drops experienced by farmers all over the country in the 1920s and 30s.

After Grandpa had given the kids a full education of the hop industry, the family was more than happy to get back in the car and drive 150 miles south on highway 99 to Portland and then on to Harrisburg, Oregon, where Grandpa's cousins, the Darlings, lived on an island on the Willamette River. Grandma said Cousin Bert was,

> . . . renting the island for 99 years and all the buildings were on stilts. He was allowed to cut down the big trees and float the logs down-river to a sawmill. They had cows and chickens on the island, and an immense garden with nut trees, and the best vegetables I have ever tasted. The garden didn't need to be watered during the summer, because the ground was soaked all winter.
>
> The Darlings also had seven children, and all the kids played together and loved the water. They had an enormous woodpile for their fuel in the winter. I told Bert about the campfires we had enjoyed at Yellowstone, which inspired him to build an even bigger campfire. Unfortunately, during the night, a spark from the fire burned up most of his woodpile.

Pauline wrote, "When we were on that island with the Darlings, we stayed for over a week. One of the girls and I were exploring the island one day when we came upon a pool of water where Keith and a Darling boy were jumping off a log into the water. They were naked!!!! We watched them, but they didn't know we were around." Decades later, my aunts and uncles thought those leisurely days on that fantasy island were some of the most memorable and joyous experiences of the trip.

After they left Harrisburg, they drove the short trip to Eugene, Oregon. Grandma wrote, "Eugene had a lovely campground, so we stayed several days while we did a good housekeeping job and rested." After they rested, the family drove directly west to the coastal road of Highway 101 and for the first time saw a long, sandy beach stretching for miles. They were finally in California and it was late August. They knew they had to find a place to live and enroll the kids in school before September.

They stayed in Crescent City on the first night and the next day drove to the Redwood Forest National Park. Today, the Redwood National and State Parks protect about 39,000 acres of old-growth forest, which is nearly half of all the remaining coastal redwoods. Some of the trees in the area have been growing for over 2,000 years, rising over 370 feet in the air. Grandma wrote, "We drove through the beautiful redwood forest. There was one tree that was so huge, it had a tunnel through which we drove the car. The loggers let us get close to where they were falling trees, which made a tremendous noise when they hit the ground."

Marilee added, "In 1972, my husband Jim and I tried to drive through the same tree, but they were charging $5 to go through, so we backed up to go around, ran into a stump, and wrecked our car."

Grandpa lined up all seven kids and Grandma around a giant redwood and took their picture with their Kodak camera. All of them, lined up hand-to-hand, barely covered half the circumference of the tree. After the Redwood Forest, they spent the night camping in Eureka, California, and then drove 270 miles on highway 101 to San Francisco.

From left to right: Grandma, Bruce, Marilee, Pauline, Gwen, Rex, Richard, Keith

Early 1930s photo of the Golden Gate Bridge. Courtesy of the Library of Congress

Grandma remembered, "We were now in San Francisco and we had to be ferried across the bay to get to town. They were almost ready to start building the Golden Gate Bridge."

The Golden Gate Bridge finally started construction on January 5, 1933, and was completed ahead of schedule in three years. The Bridge is an Art Deco suspension, truss arch bridge that spans about 1.7 miles over the Golden Gate connecting San Francisco and Marin County. Many people thought building a bridge across the 6,700-foot strait, above waters with strong, swirling tides and currents, and frequent strong winds, would be an uneven battle between man and the sea. One engineer claimed, "I know of no place on the globe which has more violent conditions of water and weather than the Golden Gate."

San Francisco is a proud city, which after their devastating earthquake and subsequent fire in 1906, rebuilt the entire city in less than nine years and presented it to the world at their 1915 Pacific-Panama Exposition. The Expo not only celebrated the rebuilding of the city, but also the opening of the Panama Canal, which the city hoped would substantially boost its shipping business.

Grandma wrote, "San Francisco was very interesting with its cable cars, Chinatown, and steep streets. Many of the Chinese wore their native clothes and pigtails. By this time, I was about ready to stop and live almost anyplace, so we hurried on to Southern California as we wanted to live close to Los Angeles."

Before the trip, Grandpa had researched all the towns around LA and found Compton was one of the best small towns with friendly neighborhoods, affordable housing, and great schools. Grandma wrote, "We drove around town and thought it was a nice, clean-looking place with good schools and good stores for shopping. The population was about 9,000. We went to a rental agency, which had a cottage for rent in a decent neighborhood, at 515 W. Poplar Street, for $20 a month. There were two bedrooms, a living room, kitchen, bathroom, and back porch, but, unfortunately, no laundry facilities. Levi and I slept in the living room and the girls occupied one bedroom and the boys the other. We bought second-hand furniture, and the landlord accepted it as a month's rent when we left."

The family was all settled in and ready to live in "Hollywoodland." The home in Compton was only fifteen miles east of the ocean community of Manhattan Beach. Zillow now shows the 601-square foot modest home looks the same as it did back in 1930, but in the summer of 2022 it was worth over $400,000.

CHAPTER EIGHT

1930–31: LIVING THE LIFE IN COMPTON, CALIFORNIA

IN LATE AUGUST 1930, AN INCREDIBLY DIRTY BLACK MODEL A FORD ROLLED INTO A QUIET COMPTON NEIGHBORHOOD FULL OF PRETTY LITTLE HOUSES POSITIONED ON LARGE LAWNS FILLED WITH BEAU-TIFUL, COLORFUL FLOWERS, AND FRUIT-LADEN TREES. As soon as the family parked next to the house, all seven kids clamored out of the car and ran around to check out their new home. The neighborhood heard the commotion and soon there were a couple dozen kids and adults who wandered over to check out the new neighbors with the Iowa license plates. As the first order of business, the family carried everything into the new house and then Grandpa made a grocery list for the week and jumped back into the car. He was very eager to get food and some soap so he could wash the car. He liked everything perfectly maintained, cleaned and in apple pie order.

Grandma stood outside for a while to soak in the sunshine, sights, and smells. She was relieved the trip had been so successful. They had traveled over 5,000 miles without a single major problem, and the kids were healthy and happy. She thought back to the sights and smells of the Iowa farms she had known all her life. She had grown used to the smells of the cows, pigs, and horses wafting about her. She had grown used to the Iowa weather. The hot, dusty, humid summers created thunderstorms, lightning, and tornadoes. How many times had she hid in the cellar when the sky turned black and green and the winds blew hard? This would be the first winter in their lives when they didn't have to worry about shoveling snow, traveling on rough, icy roads in a blizzard, and bundling all the children in heavy coats, scarves, boots, and mittens. There were no farm chores to complete, no animals to feed and care for, no clothes to make, no large home to clean, no frozen, snowy nights that needed a dozen quilts for warmth, and no need to can and freeze all that food or plow the fields. They could now take clothes to electric washers in a laundromat and didn't have to scrub them on an old washboard. This was the sabbatical, the vacation, that might save Levi from future strokes. This was the privileged opportunity they had to spend time together with their children.

Grandma later wrote,

> There was a large lawn at the house with lots of flowers and trees. We had an enormous seedless white grapevine. Some of the bunches of grapes were almost a foot long. There was also a large fig tree that lost all its leaves in the fall, so we didn't know if the figs would come back. One day in February, I noticed little knobs all over the tree. I thought they were the new leaves, but it turned out they were the new crop of figs. When

Neighborhood kids at the Compton house

the figs ripened, the neighborhood kids loved to eat them. Our gang was not too fond of the figs, but I did make fig jam that was a big hit.

We had real good neighbors and there were gobs of kids, so the kids soon found a friend. Bruce made a couple of friends named Junie and Rodney, and Gwen played with Rodney's sister, Bobbie. Junie gave Bruce her old tricycle when she got her new one for Christmas, so they rode together all over the neighborhood. Keith and Richard made scooters out of wooden boxes by attaching roller skates to the bottom of the boxes.

We had a long row of beautiful red geraniums and white calla lilies on one side of our front yard. A fresh vegetable and fruit truck came to our door every day, so we ate lots of grapefruit, oranges, and fresh vegetables. The rent was $20 a month, milk nine cents a quart, potatoes a penny a pound, bread 5 cents a loaf, hamburger 10 cents a pound, and a gallon of gas about 9 cents. Levi did the grocery shopping on Fridays as there were always many specials on that day.

To put this in perspective, at the time, 78 percent of Americans had an annual family income less than $1,500, and the depression-era unemployment rate was nearing 18 percent, so my family felt very blessed.

My grandparents had a number of choices for school for the kids. At the time, Keith was thirteen, Pauline was eleven, Richard was ten, Gwen was eight, Rex was five, Bruce was three, and Marilee was one. Grandma said, "Keith and Pauline went to Enterprise Junior High, and Richard, Rex, and Gwen went to a nearby elementary school on Orange street. The girls had to wear white middy [sailor] blouses and pleated blue serge skirts. The boys could wear whatever they wished. It was a fad for boys to wear white corduroy pants, and have their friends autograph them. Of course, they could not be washed. One mother washed them and her son was furious."

Keith was in eighth grade when he attended Enterprise Junior High, and remarked, "It was different from Iowa because we had attended a rural one-room school near our farm home. The change to a city school was very enjoyable and interesting to me."

Gwen remembered, "They set me back a grade because they thought I was too short to be in the grade I was in. We were surprised they placed students in classes by their size instead of ability. I contracted a skin disease at school and the school nurse told Mother to put a salve on it, but it got worse and wouldn't heal until one day a salesman came to the door, saw me, and told my mother to apply lard and sulphur. She did and in three days my skin was completely healed. On Sunday mornings, each one of us kids went to a different Sunday school with our friends so we had a variety of religious experiences." This acceptance of all religions ran through the core of Grandma's beliefs. When the kids were older she advised each child to "Marry someone you love and then adopt their religion." Joyous holidays at Grandma's house were always more interesting because there were a variety of religions represented.

With the older kids enrolled in school, my grandparents started to map out a plan for the next nine months. The itinerary consisted of two types of trips—events the older kids would enjoy on the weekends and events the parents would explore with the two youngest kids during school hours on weekdays. Weekend trips with the older kids would include Joshua Tree and Yosemite, Navy Day at San Pedro, and Iowa Day in Long Beach. Trips with the younger kids during the week would include destinations like Tijuana, Hemet, and missions like San Juan Capistrano. They would be busy every minute and the kids would receive a great education.

Of course, one of the first things the kids wanted to do was swim in the ocean. The closest beach was Manhattan Beach, only fifteen miles away and the LA traffic was not really that bad. They loaded up the Ford with a couple of blankets, a picnic lunch, swimsuits, and toys for the beach. The beach had a giant pier stretching out nearly 1,000 feet, with a 200-foot-long fishing extension where a number of men had their fishing rods out waiting for a catch. The bath house was located under the deck at the base of the concrete pier. It had 360 lockers for bathers and it rented swimsuits and sun umbrellas to beach goers. There were a number of old trucks on the beach selling vegetables and drinks. This beach became the family's favorite because not only was it a beautiful beach, but there was always something happening. Other beaches in the area, like Huntington Beach, were not as appealing because they were filled with dozens of monstrous oil derricks.

1930 Huntington Beach. Courtesy of Orange County Archives #1035

Every Saturday the kids would walk to the movies. They were each given ten cents for the matinee plus an extra nickel to spend. Pauline remembered, "I always bought a Sugar Daddy because it lasted so long." There were a number of interesting talking movies in 1930, including *All Quiet on the Western Front*; Howard Hughes's film *Hell's Angels*; *The Little Rascals: Best of Our Gang*; *Animal Crackers* with the Marx brothers; and *The Blue Angel* with Marlene Dietrich.

One event my grandparents looked forward to attending was a sermon by Aimee Semple McPherson, a famous Pentecostal evangelist and media celebrity. In 1922, she became the first woman to preach a sermon wirelessly. She also raised the money to build and found the giant Angelus Temple as a center of the International Church of the Foursquare Gospel. Amidst the extreme poverty and social upheaval of the time, "she passionately preached God's hope and healing power, leading countless city-wide initiatives to care for the hungry, homeless and broken," and led numerous charitable drives to help people in distress.

As the family drove through LA, they were overwhelmed by the palm trees that were casually planted everywhere in town. Grandpa explained that most of the palm trees were not native to the area. Franciscan monks who settled in Southern California in the eighteenth century, were the first ones to plant palm trees for ornamental purposes, and grape vines for Holy Communion wine. Before the 1932 Olympic Games in LA, over 40,000 Mexican fan palms were planted as part of a city-wide beautification project.

My grandparents quickly discovered that LA in 1930 was, in many ways, still part of the Wild West. Things moved fast. By 1930, LA was the fifth largest city in America, with over 1.2 million citizens in the city and over 2 million in the county. The county was virtually roiling with activity and excitement. The area was filled with wildcat oil drilling, extensive suburban development, a massive agricultural industry, and complex engineering projects including the construction of the Hoover Dam in Nevada, and the planning of a massive freeway system. A plan that assumed the "new freeway would easily handle traffic for many decades in the future." This statement brought a bit of comic relief to my research.

The LA airport had just opened and the state was deeply involved in the birth of the aircraft industry. A fifty-foot-tall Hollywoodland sign, studded with 4,000 flashing light bulbs, towered over the Hollywood Hills, earning LA the nickname, "Tinsel Town," a name that served as a metaphor for the shiny, bright, and often unreal nature of the booming Hollywoodland movie industry. Once the Depression hit, thousands of Dust Bowl refugees and the unemployed, rushed to California to find a future in this great, shiny, bright land of opportunity.

However, behind all these fast-paced accomplishments, was a soft underbelly of mafia activity, civic corruption, and religious experimentation. The 1930s *WPA Guide to Los Angeles* claimed, "The cosmopolitan populace of LA became known far and wide for its susceptibility to the teachings of sects and cults embracing such philosophies as divine healing, occult science, spiritual and mental phenomena, reincarnation, and astrological revelations."

Fortunately, my family didn't seem to be aware of the underbelly and managed to negotiate LA without any major problems. One of their first big trips was to Catalina Island.

Pauline remembered, "One weekend Dad took me, Richard, and Keith to Catalina Island. We went over on the glass bottom boat, and I got very seasick. Then we took a sight-seeing bus trip around the island. I was very impressed with the Casino." The island has a fascinating history. In 1919, William Wrigley Jr., the chewing gum heir, bought most of the shares of the Santa Catalina Island Company, and then invested millions on his vision to create "a playground for all," which included infrastructure, a reservoir, the Hotel Atwater, Bird Park, and the famous Catalina Casino.

Surprisingly, the twelve-story Art Deco and Mediterranean Revival style Casino, which stands proudly on its regal perch on the edge of Avalon Bay, never had gambling. Instead, the building contained the Avalon Theatre on the main floor, which was one of the first movie theatres equipped for "talking movies." Also inside, was a five-story lavish ballroom, with the world's largest circular post-free dance floor, which could hold up to 1,500 dancers. Later the Wrigley family deeded most of the land to the Catalina Island Conservancy, creating the oldest and largest private land trust in Southern California.

One of the next adventures was attending the four-day celebration of Navy Day in San Pedro. On Thursday, October 30, the whole family piled into the Ford and drove about fifteen miles south to the naval base in San Pedro. Thousands attended the event, which included planes taking off and landing from navy ships, tours of ships, and other events. At one point, the family was lined up to watch a navy plane take off from the USS Idaho aircraft carrier. Pauline later noted, "We went aboard an aircraft carrier and watched them launch planes from the deck. One plane capsized and two boys were drowned." I read my aunt's statement with some doubts about the memory of an eleven-year child. Did this really happen? So I did some research and found her memory was just fine.

I found a 1930 article from the *Wilmington Daily Press*, that revealed the navy plane plunged into the water after takeoff. A Japanese fishing boat was nearby and one of its fishermen dived out of his boat and swam down in the dark waters to release one of the pilots, Lt. Anderson, from the plane. Unfortunately, both pilots were killed in the crash. The fisherman was given a Carnegie Medal for his attempt to save the pilots' lives. The sight of this tragedy stayed with the family for years as Grandma watched six of her thirteen children march off to World War II, and was poignant for Pauline, as decades later, two of her children became navy fighter pilots. They saw first-hand the potential dangers of war.

During the Navy Days, Grandpa was thrilled to learn that he could charter a ride on an airplane at the LAX airport. The old 1930 pictures of the airport revealed that it was filled with bi-planes, which had two layers of wings, so it is likely that grandpa flew on a bi-plane. The new airport was dedicated in June of 1930, during which Mines Field was renamed the Los Angeles Municipal Airport (LAX). At the two-day

1930 LA Airport. Courtesy of LA Chamber of Commerce and USC Libraries

gala event, 65,000 spectators jammed the field for the air races. LAX was used by private pilots and flying schools, but the commercial flights were out of the Glendale and Burbank airports. LAX didn't have commercial airline service until 1946.

Grandpa had hoped he could get a plane ride in the mid-1920s when a barnstormer named Charles Lindberg had scheduled an exhibition in Forest City, but it was canceled due to severe thunderstorms. Grandpa was disappointed because the Lindberg fellow and his buddies were famous for aerial acrobatics, walking on the wings, and parachute jumping. Pauline wrote, "In LA, Dad took a ride in an airplane, but he would not let anyone else go. He always thought about us and wanted either mom or him to be left with us in case something happened." Grandpa had a great time on the flight, but the kids were very jealous they couldn't go along.

The adventures continued. One fall day in 1930, my grandparents were inside their home preparing a meal, when they heard a distant boom. They ran outside and saw a large dark plume of smoke rising in the sky. Their next-door neighbor and good friend, Eddie Hanks, who worked in the oil fields, was also standing outside his home looking at the

Fighting Oil Fire in Late 1920s.
Courtesy of the Gerth Archives and Special Collection, CSU Dominguez Hills

dark plume. He yelled to my grandpa, "An oil rig must have exploded, let's jump in the car and go look." This is what men do. When they see a giant explosion a few miles away, they will jump in the car and go look. Women and children, most generally, seek a safer path and stay home.

It is somewhat surprising to a newcomer that in 1930, LA produced nearly one-fourth of the world's oil output. A 1926 *Los Angeles Times* article bragged, "The Standard Oil Company of California is the largest individual producer of crude oil in the US and dominates the marketing of petroleum products along the west coast of both Americas."

The history of oil production in California runs deep. By 1897, LA already had 500 derricks, and by 1910 the area near Santa Monica Boulevard and Vermont Avenue was an unruly oil shantytown. Drilling activity reached new heights in the 1920s when major finds were made in Whittier, Montebello, Compton, Torrance, and Inglewood. Even now, there are still over 3,000 active wells remaining in LA county, and over 7 million people currently live within a mile of an oil or gas well.

When Richard and Keith were in school, they learned there were hundreds of dinosaur fossils, located just a few miles north of Compton in the La Brea Tar Pits and Hancock Park. If you have been a parent of thirteen and ten-year-old boys, you know they will keep nagging until you finally capitulate and show them the dinosaur bones. Grandpa loaded the boys in the car and headed for the Tar Pits. The boys were mesmerized as they examined the fossils of saber-toothed cats, wolves, and giant wooly mammoths that used to roam the very land they were standing on. The Tar Pits is the only actively excavated Ice Age fossil site in the world located in an urban setting and discoveries are still being made in the area. In 2006, when the LA County Museum of Art began the construction of an underground parking garage, fossils were discovered from a near-complete Columbian mammoth. To this day, the staff are still salvaging what they call "Project 23."

However, the women had their own favorite excavations—shopping at the Mays Department Store. The men stayed home and watched the kids, while the wives went to downtown LA to shop. Grandma remembered she took her first escalator ride at Mays. The giant ten-story building on the corners of Broadway, 8th and Hill, was a perfect place for all their Christmas shopping. The imposing structure with its terra-cotta facades was a familiar part of the bustling downtown LA shopping district. According to the 1930 store directory, one could shop for most anything—appliances, furniture, sporting goods, clothing, beauty treatments, jewelry, and office machines. Grandma bought socks, pajamas, and other clothing for Christmas presents and also found a few inexpensive toys and games that would be fun for the kids to unwrap.

In early December, Grandpa found a nice small tree and bought a few lights and some "tinsel" for decoration. It seemed so weird to put up a Christmas tree on a sunny 80-degree day. Without doubt, LA was an easy, fun, and beautiful place to live.

During Christmas vacation, the family decided to travel to Joshua Tree. They took the route through Anaheim on old Highway 99 and up the Twentynine Palms road. It was only about 130 miles to Joshua Tree, but the trip lasted all day and seemed like it took forever. The area has been described as a "lifeless wasteland," holding the twisted and formidable-looking Joshua trees sparsely scattered around the region. The tree is the largest species of yucca and can live for hundreds of years and grows to about forty feet tall. It takes hours to drive through the desert park and it is rare to see a lot of people or cars. It was a lonely journey with few gas stations or park facilities along the route, although the town of Twentynine Palms was a booming health resort at the time. It's worth the trip to venture deep in the park because one of the lookouts is so elevated and spectacular, you can see Mexico with the naked eye. A conservationist named Minerva Hoyt lobbied for years in the 1920s and 1930s to make Joshua Tree the first national desert park. She finally persuaded President Roosevelt to make the park an official national monument in 1936, but it didn't become a national park until 1994. In 2012, the US Board of Geographic Names voted to name a mountain peak after Minerva for all her efforts in establishing the park.

After settling back after their trip to Joshua Tree, the family experienced a signature LA event: an earthquake. They were sitting on the living room couch, when it suddenly started sliding across the room. It was a small rumbling quake that did little damage, but the family was thrilled to experience the event. They decided that a few little quakes seemed much better than the tornadoes that roared through Iowa every year. A couple of years later, they changed their minds, when in March of 1933, a magnitude 6.4 earthquake hit the cities of Long Beach and Compton. Within a few seconds, over 100 people were killed and 120 schools in the area were damaged or destroyed because of the unreinforced masonry bearing walls. Some of the schools were ones the kids had attended. Recently, the US Geological Survey completed new studies that identified evidence that the 1933 earthquake was likely caused by deep drilling in oil fields at Huntington Beach.

The biggest event of the new year of 1931 was the Iowa Day Picnic. The first Iowa Picnic was on January 1, 1886 at Lincoln Park, when 400 Iowans got together to celebrate the ability to actually have a picnic in January. It was started by a group of Iowa farmers who had retired from farming and decided to spend the rest of their lives spreading the gospel of eternal sunshine and good living. For some reason they all ended up living around Long Beach. By 1930, the *LA Times* declared the picnic had grown to 125,000 attendees and the town of Long Beach had earned the nickname, "Iowa by the Sea." There were so many Iowans in attendance that they had to divide up into groups based on which of the 99 Iowa counties they had lived in.

The Iowans were entertained with bands, late-night dancing, picnics, and singing. Their favorite song was, "That's Where the Tall Corn Grows": "We're from I-o-way, I-o-way. State of all the land. Joy in ev'ry hand. We're from I-o-way. I-o-way. That's where the tall corn grows."

The Iowans would belt out the song and then stand with their hands held high whenever they sang—Tall Corn Grows. The *Long Beach Post News* in 1930 (written by the *Des Moines Register's* "Over the Coffee" columnist, Harlan Miller), revealed how these retired Iowa farmers lived. "Many of them live on $60-70 a month. $30 would go to rent, $25 for food and clothing, $10 for medicine and doctors, and $10 for riotous living." A typical day for the transplanted farmers would begin with a game of horseshoes at the park and continue with a stroll around Rainbow Pier. From 2:30 to 4 p.m. they would attend the afternoon concert on the beach, and then have dinner at a nearby restaurant for thirty-five to sixty cents. After dinner, they would walk around window shopping on Pine Street, and then dance until 2:00 a.m.

In 1928, when Iowan Herbert Hoover was running for president, he spoke at the Iowa picnic hoping to win those 100,000-plus Iowa votes. Iowa attendees wore red ribbons for Iowa natives and white ribbons if you had lived in Iowa for over fifty years. In 1950, California governor Earl Warren famously proclaimed, "We have more Iowans here in southern California than they have in the whole state of Iowa." In 1920, a direct rail line was established from Des Moines to the Terminal Island of Long Beach. The cost of a one-way ticket was only $5. Grandma couldn't resist turning to Grandpa and teasing, "You mean we could have gotten here in a couple of days for $5?"

One day my grandparents and their Iowa friends, the Hagens, decided to splurge and have lunch at the famous Brown Derby restaurant at 3427 Wilshire Boulevard, which was shaped like a giant brown derby hat. The place, a haven for movie stars, was where careers were made, contracts signed, and ideas pitched within the confines of the numbered, leather booths. My grandparents were thrilled to sit in the restaurant and wait for the movie stars to pour in while they ate their hamburgers. The meal was expensive; according to a 1930 menu, the cheeseburgers and lettuce salads were twenty-five cents each.

In the spring of 1931, Grandma took some of the kids to a local park. There were dozens of kids at the park with their parents, when she noticed officials were questioning and arresting a number of men. Grandma started asking around and learned that government agents from the Department of Labor and the Bureau of Immigration were in the process of rounding up over 400,000 Mexican Americans in LA, many of whom were full US citizens, and deporting them back to Mexico. In the 1920s, before the Depression, when jobs were plentiful and workers were needed for non-skilled labor, the Mexicans were more than welcome. However, when the Depression wore on and thousands of unemployed people were streaming into California to find jobs, the government decided these new American citizens were no longer wanted. There were newspaper reports of Mexican American families whose fathers never came home. It was assumed the men were deported, even though the fathers were citizens of this country. Grandma, a first-generation born citizen, was horrified. She remembered vividly during World War I, there were some politicians in Iowa who hated Germans so much, they wanted to deport or confine German immigrants in the state. What would she have done if the government had decided to deport her father or other members of her family? How would the family have survived? She decided she wanted to go to Mexico to see what was happening with the Mexican Americans.

On one particularly sunny day in early spring, the family wound their way down the coastal ocean road to get to Mexico. The endless beach had a long succession of big ocean resort hotels gleaming in the sun, surrounded by tropical blooming seacoast gardens. But the glamor of the ocean resorts soon disappeared as they crossed the border to Mexico and discovered something even more stunning—the Agua Caliente Casino.

From 1919 to 1933, alcohol, casinos, prostitution, and horse racing were all forbidden or tightly restricted in California, but they were a growth industry in Tijuana, Mexico. A giant pleasure palace called the Agua Caliente Casino was built and Hollywood celebrities and the wealthy raced to the scene. *The Los Angeles Times* concluded, "There isn't another place on the continent, outside of a US mint, where you can see so much money piled up before your eyes at one time. Its only rival in the world is Monte Carlo." The casino was only six miles south of the border, covered 655 acres, and cost about $10 million—a handsome sum at the time. The casino sported a horse-racing track, a golf course, a spa, an Art Deco ballroom, cocktail bars, tennis courts, and a landing strip for small planes. The showroom featured a teenage dancer, Margarita Cansino, who later changed her name to Rita Hayworth. *Architectural Digest* did a sixteen-page feature story on the complex and Hollywood filmed a movie based on the casino, called *"In Caliente."* However, when Prohibition ended in 1933, people turned to Las Vegas for their casino adventures.

My grandparents didn't drink, smoke, race horses, gamble, golf, or play tennis so they were awe-struck by the entire concept. They quickly surveyed the rest of Tijuana and drove back to safety in Compton.

The family's next weekend trip involved driving north rather than south. Grandma had heard so much about the beauty of the flowers in the city of Santa Barbara, that she had to go see it. Some people thought the city reminded them of the beautiful ocean gardens in southern France and Monte Carlo. Grandma was a prize-winning gardener who specialized in flowers. Every summer I stayed at Grandma's house in Crystal Lake, attended the local horticulture shows, and Grandma's flowers nearly always won blue ribbons.

The hundred-mile drive to Santa Barbara followed highway 101 curving in and out of bays each lovelier than the last. The city was filled with elegant white stucco buildings with bright red/orange tile roofs. The highways were lined with orange, lemon, walnut, and olive groves. The pale pink roses, succulents, gerbera daisies, tulips, and lilies appeared in lush gardens, filling the air with the most exquisite smells. Grandma bought some flower seeds, and decided that if she had another daughter, she would be named Barbara, after the colorful city she loved so much.

Their next road trip was to Hemet to see the Ramona Pageant play. Hemet lies in the San Jacinto Valley surrounded by the Santa Rosa Hills and the San Jacinto Mountains. They took their friends, the Wilson family from Forest City, and headed east. Helen Hunt Jackson, the author of the play, became one of the leading advocates for Native American Indian rights. She researched the broken treaties, brutal murders, and deceptive government policies imposed on the Native American people, and documented them in her 1881 book entitled, *A Century of Dishonor*. The book did not catch on, so she wrote the story of Ramona in the form of a play, hoping that an emotional story would be more convincing than her documented research. In May of 2023, the play will celebrate its hundredth anniversary, still performing at Hemet's outdoor amphitheater. The play is akin to the *Great Gatsby* and *Romeo and Juliet*, and offers a glimpse of the tragic history of Southern California's native people.

In the spring after the snow in the mountains melted, the family decided to drive the 300 miles to Yosemite National Park. On the way, they drove through the Sierra Nevada Mountains to see the Sequoia National Park and the General Grant National Park. The tiny Grant Park was created in 1890 for the purpose of preserving the second tallest sequoia tree, which had been named for General Grant. Ten years after my family visited Grant Park, the US acquired 720 square acres in the area and created the Kings Canyon National Park, which included Grant Park. The Sequoia trees in the parks can live more than 2,000 years, but usually die from fires or toppling from their own height and weight. Their roots are shallow and without a taproot reaching far into the ground, the wet soil and strong winds can easily topple them.

The Yosemite National Park is located a few miles north of Sequoia and Kings Canyon. In 1903, John Muir and President Theodore Roosevelt camped under the stars at Glacier Point in Yosemite and the president declared, "It was like lying in a great solemn cathedral, far vaster and more beautiful than any built by the hands of man." Muir may have arrived at the park as a "nobody," but his passion for the beauty of the national parks and his fights to save them, made him the co-founder and president of the Sierra Club, a renowned writer, an activist naturalist, and a catalyst for the creation of Yosemite, Sequoia, Mount Rainier, and Grand Canyon national parks. His hard work and passion earned him the sobriquet of "Father of the National Parks." While at the park, the family also saw photographs by another naturalist and advocate, Ansel Adams, who first photographed Yosemite in 1927.

The kids loved the ancient sequoia trees, Bridalveil Fall Trail, and the Half Dome. However, their favorite was the granite cliffs of the great El Capitan, but they just couldn't figure out how to climb the nearly vertical edifice, so Grandpa had to show them other trails to hike. Their favorite tree in the park was a giant sequoia called the Wawona Tunnel tree, which had a tunnel carved in it, so the car could drive right through the tree. The tunnel was carved in 1881 for the purpose of increasing tourism, but decades later it was discovered tunneling actually made the tree more vulnerable. In 1969, the tree, heavy with winter snow, toppled over and died. The national parks no longer allow tunnels to be built through the large trees.

In March 1931, Grandma wrote a letter back to her mother in Webster City, and mentioned she had "baked" a devil's food cake in her pressure cooker and it turned out fine. The cake must have been made for Marilee's second birthday on March 23, because it was the only spring birthday in the family. Grandma also wrote more about the rambunctious two-year-old. "Marilee can talk and she sure is a little pest. She likes to be outdoors all the time, but we have to watch her or she will be in the middle of the street."

The family also enjoyed touring the many missions in southern California. Their favorite was the Mission at San Juan Capistrano in Orange County. It was founded in the late 1700s as the seventh of twenty-one statewide missions, and features a chapel that is still standing. The miracle of the "Swallows" of Capistrano takes place each year at the Mission on March 19, when the birds fly back home from all parts of the world.

And just like the swallows who flew back every year to their home in Capistrano, so did the Iowa snowbirds need to drive back to their home in Iowa. It was late May, school was out, and they were once again loading up the Ford to explore more of the country and wing their way back to Forest City, Iowa.

CHAPTER NINE

1931: HOME TO IOWA

IT WAS EARLY SUMMER, SCHOOL WAS OUT, AND THE SNOWBIRDS WERE READY TO RETURN TO IOWA. They packed up the car and said goodbye to all the neighbors and friends. Most of the kids were eager to get home to Iowa, excited to see more national parks, but not too excited about the 5,000-plus mile trip back home.

The trip home would go through the Mojave Desert, the Grand Canyon, and a number of national parks in Utah. They would drive through Arizona, Nevada, Idaho, Colorado, New Mexico, Texas, Oklahoma, Tennessee, Arkansas, and Missouri. Not exactly the most direct route back to Iowa, but it allowed for stops to see relatives and a lot of interesting areas around the country.

The first leg of the return trip involved crossing two hundred miles over the impossibly scorched, monochromatic, blistering, and isolated Mojave Desert to get to Needles, California. They took Route 66, also called the Will Rogers Highway, The Main Street of America, and the

Mother Road. The highway, cobbled together in the 1920s, traversed 2,448 miles from Santa Monica to Chicago, and is one of this country's most famous roads, made legendary through pop culture and Dust Bowl history. The family traveled at night across the Mohave Desert, because it would have been prohibitive to cross it during the day with the hot summer sun beating down on a car with nine people and no air conditioning.

Once they arrived at the small town of Needles, they were intrigued to see El Garces, a Harvey House restaurant managed by the famous Fred Harvey. The town was an important stop for the Atchison, Topeka, and Santa Fe Railway, so when the original depot burned down in 1906, the railroad spared no expense on the replacement facility. It was finished in 1908 and built to look like a Greek temple.

The Harvey House was a western US restaurant-hotel chain famous in the late nineteenth century until the mid-twentieth century. They built their facilities in key depots along the railways, including many on the Atchison, Topeka, and Santa Fe routes. They were famous for their superior quality of food and service. The "waitresses" were called Harvey Girls—made more famous by the 1940s Judy Garland movie called *The Harvey Girls*. These popular facilities, built west of the Mississippi, were so well managed and well received, they were known as the "Civilizer of the West."

Grandma wrote that after they left Needles, they drove a hundred miles north to the Boulder Dam in Nevada. When I first read this, I thought Grandma was wrong—the dam outside of Las Vegas is called Hoover Dam. But as usual, Grandma was right. The dam was called the Boulder Canyon Project when it was built from 1928 to 1936. The name Hoover Dam was approved by Congress in 1947, as an honorific for President Hoover. The dam impounds Lake Mead, the largest reservoir in the US by volume when full. It is a concrete arch-gravity dam in the Black Canyon of the Colorado River on the border of Nevada and Arizona, directly east of Las Vegas.

Grandma wrote, "The Dam was under construction and it did not seem possible someday the area would be a big lake. The drive to the

Dam site was an easy downhill drive, but coming back up was another matter. Several cars couldn't make it and were stalled along the way. Our Ford just chugged along. It was terribly hot down by the river—too hot to walk around. If you wanted a drink of water, it cost ten cents a glass, so we carried our own water." Grandma was right about the heat. The summer of 1931 was especially torrid in the area, with daytime highs averaging 120 degrees. When the dam was finished it reached the height of a sixty-story building and held the world's largest turbines and generators.

After the dam adventure, they caught Route 66 and turned south on old Highway 89 to Phoenix and then Flagstaff for dinner and camping for the night. The kids were very excited, because the next day they would get to see the Grand Canyon National Park.

In the morning after breakfast, they piled into the Ford and traveled through the beautiful Painted Desert, a badlands in northwest Arizona that wraps around the northwestern edges of the Petrified Forest, which became a national park in 1962. The desert has endless colorful, horizontally stripped, flat-topped mesas and sculptured buttes. After leaving the Painted Desert and driving through miles of dense pine, my family was shocked when suddenly the Canyon appeared directly before them without warning. They drove along the South Rim, occasionally stopping to observe the "Divine Abyss."

After a couple miles, they found themselves right next to the El Tovar Hotel on the south edge of the Grand Canyon. The Atchison, Topeka, and Santa Fe Railway built the hotel in 1905 as a destination place for their wealthy clients, and the famous Harvey House operated the restaurant and hotel. When the railway originally designed the hotel, it was supposed to be cantilevered right over the edge of the vast chasm of the canyon. It would have been a stunning view for the hotel guests, but would have destroyed the experience for everyone else. Fortunately, some reason took over and the hotel was built twenty feet back from the canyon rim. The El Tovar was one of the first such hotels built in national parks, part of a trend in which railroads, in order to

1905 El Tovar hotel at Grand Canyon. Courtesy of the National Park Service

attract wealthy tourists, would build large hotels in newly accessible scenic locations like the Yellowstone and Glacier National Parks.

The chief architect for the Harvey House company was Mary Colter, who designed the hotel interiors and many of the buildings on the South Rim. Her reputation grew fast because of her use of natural materials in forms that mimicked nature. Her unique style served as the basis for what we now term "rustic" architecture.

At the turn of the century, the Grand Canyon was also facing the same existential crisis as Yellowstone and other parks. The US government had pushed out the Hualapai and Havasupai Indian tribes so that mining and logging companies might have their way with the canyon and pine forest. A number of mining companies had permits to explore the area looking for minerals, gold or whatever they could find. The logging companies were clear-cutting the woods, and anyone could set up a stand and sell mule rides, souvenirs, and food. The railroad was in competition with all these stakeholders to see who could prosper the most from the land. No one was in charge.

In 1903, before the Grand Canyon was a formally protected park, President Theodore Roosevelt paid a visit, stood on the rim of the canyon, and gave a famous and impassioned speech:

I want to ask you to do one thing in connection with
it [Grand Canyon] in your own interest and in the
interest of the country—to keep this great wonder of
nature as it is now. I hope you will not have a building
of any kind, not a summer cottage, a hotel or anything
else, to mar the wonderful grandeur, the sublimity,
the great loveliness and beauty of the canyon. Leave it
as it is. You cannot improve upon it.

This speech must have terrified the Atchison, Topeka, and Santa
Fe, which was in the process of designing the El Tovar Hotel as well as
railroad tracks across the park. The hotel was named after the Spanish
conquistador, Don Pedro de Tovar, who "discovered" the canyon in 1540
and immediately reported it to his boss, Francisco Vasquez de Coronado.
In less than two years after Roosevelt's speech, both the hotel and the
railroad tracks through the park were quickly built. It was no small task
to build a luxury hotel about a hundred miles from a dependable source
of water. Rail cars shipped water to the site and stored it in the turret on
top of the hotel, which housed a 10,000-gallon storage tank. One can still
take a train ride from Williams, Arizona, through the park, right to the
El Tovar, twenty feet from the rim of the canyon.

The promotional ads for the hotel and the canyon encouraged tourists "To see how the world was made . . . deep down in the earth a mile
or more you go past strata of every known geologic age. All glorified
by a rainbow beauty of color." The LA Times gushed about the hotel,
"Reared upon the very brink of the dizzy gulf of the gorge, the view
afforded the guests from its windows and balconies is something to live
long uneffaced in the memory." Fortunately, The Grand Canyon was
proclaimed a National Monument in 1908, the National Park Service
was created in 1916, and the Grand Canyon National Park was finally
established by Congress in 1919. But what if that hadn't happened?
What would the parks have looked like now? Roosevelt wasn't able to
stop the building of the El Tovar, but he was effective in setting aside

more than 230 million acres of wild America for posterity. His executive orders not only saved the Devils Tower, the Grand Canyon, and the Petrified Forest from more unplanned development, but he helped make conservation a universal and popular endeavor.

Naturalist John Burroughs described the canyon as the "Divine Abyss where one looks into the earth as through a mighty window or open door." Grandma wrote, "The Grand Canyon was a wonderful place with good camping areas. There were lots of people there. While standing on the rim of the canyon, the Colorado River looked like a silver ribbon stretched along the bottom. I was overwhelmed at the sight, as it was so beautiful, and the colors changed several times a day." The family marveled at the lightning and rainstorms barreling through the canyon, leaving sparkling, full rainbows in their wake. As Grandma looked into the steep abyss, she, like many of us, realized that no matter what tragedies are imposed upon your life, they will go away or be resolved. When staring at a marvel of nature that took millions of years to create, one is gripped with the knowledge that the problems we have today are minor and fleeting compared to the permanence of God's great creations.

For many years the "Bright Angel Trail" on the North Rim of the Canyon was privately owned, and tourists paid to ride a mule down to the Colorado River. The owner of the Trail was US Congressman Cameron, who was also claiming mining rights to most of the South Rim, including the land under El Tovar. In 1914, William Randolph Hearst bought one of the remaining South Rim properties and let it be known that he was building his own hotel. He also announced he was becoming an Arizona citizen and running for the US Senate. These were some of the many reasons why Congress was so slow to make the Canyon a park supervised by a national park service.

When the El Tovar was built on the South Rim, the railroad, in order to attract tourist dollars, built a new mule trail right next to the hotel. When my family arrived at the hotel, they quickly decided they would all take the mule ride down the canyon. The kids were experienced at riding horses, so they showed no fear as they slowly descended

Grand Canyon

more than 5,000 feet to the Colorado River. While descending, Keith and Richard were riding mules side by side, with Richard riding precariously near the edge of the mile-high abyss. Suddenly, a rattlesnake made a lunge at Richard's mule. With one hand and herculean strength, Keith grabbed Richard, hurled him over his mule, and set him down on the other side of the path. Keith said he never again was able to repeat that daring feat, but it may have saved my dad's life.

After the trip on the mules, the family spent some time exploring the El Tovar Hotel, which appeared to be a cross between a dark wood log cabin castle and a Swiss chateau, decorated with the occasional Indian rugs and moose heads. The nearby Hopi House, also designed by Mary Colter, was modeled after the 1,000-year-old pueblo dwellings of the Hopi village, and designed as an "Indian Arts Building"—a moniker applied to the railroad's souvenir shops.

After leaving the Grand Canyon, Grandpa continued across the Painted Desert and drove over Grand Canyon Bridge (now called the Navajo Bridge), which at the time was the highest in the world at 800 feet long and 485 feet above the raging Colorado River. In the 1930s, this bridge connected Arizona with Utah on the famous old trail made by the Mormons and connected the North Rim of the Grand Canyon with Bryce and Zion National Parks in Utah.

The massive canyons in the national parks are formed by three basic movements: the movement of rivers, the processes of weathering and erosion, and tectonic activity. The Grand Canyon is a product of tectonic uplift, carved over millions of years, as the Colorado River scissored its way down through the Colorado Plateau. Zion National Park's rock layers have been uplifted, tilted, and eroded to form what is called the Grand Staircase, a series of colorful cliffs between Bryce and Zion.

The name Zion is Hebrew for Jerusalem and Arabic for Holy Sanctuary. The red rock canyon at Zion, was carved by the North Fork of the Virgin River. The park has four life zones: desert, riparian (river banks), woodland, and coniferous forest. Grandma thought

Bryce Canyon

the vegetation was very much like the middle west, including the box elder trees.

After Zion, the family drove to Bryce Canyon, which is a red-rock wonderland created by wind, water, and snow erosion. When looking down into this giant amphitheater, one sees a battalion of colorful rocky spires called "hoodoos." Grandma wrote that she and Grandpa walked down the path deep in the canyon, but had a tougher walk back up. She wrote, "When I got back to the top, I dropped on my stomach and laid there for some time to get my breath. The vegetation along the path was beautiful, but there were just too many steps, and it was hot. At night the canyon looked really spooky—sort of a grayish color, and I felt that a ghost could appear from behind a rock. There was a nice campground so we stayed a couple of days."

Decades later when visiting Bryce, Kerry and I stayed at a 110-year old cabin near the edge of the canyon and marveled at the darkness and lack of ambient light. The park ranger told us, it was so dark, you could see the space station with the naked eye, 254 miles up in the sky.

After their adventures in Bryce and Zion, the family woke up bright and early, had breakfast and broke camp to make the 170-mile drive on Highway 89 to Salt Lake City, Utah. Grandma wrote, "The streets in Salt Lake were very wide and everything was well taken care of." However, the family was not too impressed with the Great Salt Lake, as it was dried up, messy, and the water was very salty. This didn't stop Grandpa, thirteen-year-old Keith, and my ten-year-old dad, Richard, because they all jumped in the lake and had a grand time floating in the salty sea. The Great Salt Lake was a freshwater inland sea of less than thirty-five feet in depth, with an outlet to the Pacific Ocean through the Snake River. The lake has evaporated even more in the twenty-first century to a point where it is now nine times saltier than the ocean.

Grandma enjoyed the Saltair dance pavilion, a massive mosque-looking resort built on 2,000 posts and pilings, cantilevered over the lake. The first building was destroyed by fire in 1925, but a new pavilion was built on the same location, which claimed to have the largest dance floor in the world. In 1933, two years after the family saw it, the resort was left high and dry when the lake waters dramatically receded. In 1970, it was destroyed by an arson fire.

Grandma also liked the Tabernacle, a large oval-shaped domed building near the Temple. The Tabernacle had such extraordinary acoustics that you could hear a pin drop from a distance of 250 feet. Grandma wrote, "While going through the Tabernacle grounds, I saw beehives placed everywhere. I asked a guard why? His reply was, 'If we keep our young people as busy as bees, they have no time to get into trouble.' I thought that was a very good idea. Our kids always had something to do."

After Salt Lake City, they drove about 340 miles south and east to Montrose, Colorado, through the Black Canyon of the Gunnison National Park. Grandpa had a cousin there, but when the family arrived, their daughter refused to believe Levi was her cousin and would not let him in the house. Fortunately, she did let the family camp for the night in their yard, but my grandparents felt so uncomfortable and embarrassed that they left early in the morning. It was so shocking to the family that all the cousins had been so happy to see them, except this one family. My grandparents put a high premium on being kind and considerate to all people, and this cousin did not pass the test.

After the short trip to Montrose, they made their way on Highway 50 about 340 miles northeast to Denver, Colorado. They passed through the Continental Divide at Monarch Pass, elevation 11,386 feet, and drove on to the Royal Gorge in Canon City. The Royal Gorge bridge took less than six months to build in 1929 for what became the highest and most famous suspension bridge in America. The bridge spans 1,260 feet across the gorge and showcases miles of scenery equaled in few places on the globe. The bridge is suspended from immense steel supports buried in the granite walls on either side and swings 956 feet above the wild Arkansas River.

The family found a good camping place near Canon City by Pueblo and were thrilled when Grandpa came back with two dozen roasting ears of corn that cost thirty cents. The next leg of trip involved a short drive north on Highway 85 to Denver, which was the twenty-ninth most populated city in America in 1931. They had planned to stay at the famous Overland Motor Park, the biggest in the country, which had opened in 1922 and covered 160 acres. The park boasted of free amenities to guests including a soda fountain, grocery store, laundry room, pool table, and filling station all surrounding a massive three-story club house. However, when they arrived, they found the park to be in bad shape with not many amenities. The Depression had deepened and the vacationing tourist campers had been replaced by homeless people looking for shelter. Despite this, Grandma thought Denver had, "Lovely trees, parks, and flowers. The Capital Building was gorgeous and the US Mint building was one of my favorite places."

Later that year, the weather turned dry and formed the beginnings of the most widespread and longest lasting droughts in Colorado history and the beginning of the Dust Bowl. By 1933, it was estimated that 25 percent of the Denver population was unemployed and hundreds of farmers and others were streaming into Denver to find work.

There is some evidence the family may have gone up to see Estes Park, Colorado, and the Rocky Mountain National Park. The Rockies are the main artery of providing water to the area. Snow collects in the rugged peaks and when it melts, creates the alpine lakes and streams that flow into the surrounding rivers. These lakes and rivers supplied water for one quarter of this country. Estes Park had its own existential crisis when Britain's Earl of Dunraven, of Yellowstone big-game hunting fame, fell in love with Estes. In 1874, he claimed about 15,000 acres of the park for his private and exclusive use as a game reserve. He accomplished this magical feat by stretching the provisions of the Homestead Act and pre-emption rights. He found a number of people who would make 160-acre claims on the land and then sell them back to Dunraven for $5 an acre. He ended up with 8,200 acres of land and another 7,000 acres of springs and streams. The legal battles lasted for decades, until the Earl finally gave up and Estes Park was formally open to the public.

After leaving Colorado, the family headed west at Pueblo through the Great Sand Dunes National Park towards Santa Fe, which was founded in 1607. It might seem like it could be the oldest city in the country, but the oldest is St. Augustine, Florida, founded in 1565. Santa Fe was filled with historic buildings and the culture of the Spanish as well as the native American tribes. For example, the Palace of the Governors was reconstructed from an ancient Indian Pueblo building in 1605, even before the Pilgrims landed in New Amsterdam, Jamestown, and Plymouth Rock. For over three centuries it was used as an executive building by the Spanish and other settlers and is recognized as a gem of early Spanish Architecture. The popular San Miguel Church was built sometime between 1541 and 1607 and reigns as the oldest Catholic church in America and is still used regularly for religious services.

Grandma, an avid plant lover, was also impressed with the cacti in the area including the yuccas and saguaros. She described the saguaro as "a tall, ungainly looking plant-tree which is ninety percent water. A big two-hundred-year-old saguaro may hold enough for up to a two-year supply of water."

The family stopped at the Palace of the Governor's museum and saw old guns, bows and arrows, pottery, arrow heads, and many other

1930 Santa Fe La Fonda Hotel.
Courtesy of Historic Hotels of America and the National Trust for Historic Preservation

relics. The family was awed by the architecture in Santa Fe, especially the La Fonda Hotel, rebuilt in 1922 in downtown Santa Fe. The architect, Isaac Rapp, was often called the "Creator of the Santa Fe Style," a Spanish Colonial Revival style architecture. In 1925, the building was acquired by the Atchison, Topeka and Santa Fe Railway and leased to Fred Harvey. When they took over, Harvey asked architect Mary Colter to recreate the inside of the building as a luxurious Harvey House.

As the family stopped to look at the La Fonda Hotel, dozens of vividly costumed Navajos and Hopis were outside performing their native ceremonial songs and dances. Their blankets and long braids were woven with red cloth and their headbands, beads, and silver ornaments gave a festive flair to the ceremony. My grandparents were so captivated about their performance and culture, that they decided to drive up to Taos to see their community.

The Hopi Indians lived on a reservation near Taos, and had blankets and pottery for sale to tourists. Grandma wrote the "Hopis had lived in that area for longer than any other surviving people. It had been a long, hard struggle for them to hold onto their land. They were very friendly and we bought several blankets and pottery jars from them."

After leaving Taos, they drove to the nearby Puye cliff dwellings carved into the mountains. It was the home to hundreds of Pueblo Indians who lived, farmed, and hunted in the area between 900 and 1580 AD. The site was excavated in 1907 and you could see the giant holes carved in the mountain and the homemade ladders reaching up to each layer of housing. However, they were charging fifty cents a person for the up-close tour, so the family decided to pass and proceeded to drive 300 miles southeast to Texas.

When driving across the Texas Panhandle, they could see cotton fields and oil wells surrounding the well-paved roads. They spent the night in Amarillo and then drove 365 miles to Dallas, stopping at Wichita Falls and Fort Worth. On the way from Fort Worth to Dallas there were oil wells, big grain fields and millions of bluebonnets, the state flower. The Dallas area was different and "bigger" than any place they had been. The big event in the town was the grand opening of the Simms Super Service Station at the corner of Cedar Springs and Maple, close to Victory Park. The *Dallas Morning News* excitedly wrote, "the filling station will be equipped with ten electrically operated gasoline pumps, every kind of automobile repair, and battery and tire vulcanizing services." Vulcanizing is the process for hardening rubber for rubber hoses, erasers, conveyor belts, tires, and bowling balls.

Grandma reflected back on the unique culture of all the cities they had visited—the food, the architecture, and the sensibilities of the people who lived there. Los Angeles was energetic and business revolved around Hollywood, agriculture, and the oil wells. The city had palm trees, lovely weather, and a casual beach atmosphere. The food was a combination of Mexican, Japanese, and casual fast food. Santa Fe had unique Spanish architecture, with a lot of Native American influence. The Salt Lake City culture was centered around the Mormon religion and the giant Salt Lake. Dallas had a large downtown area with tall buildings, lots of barbeque, and the legendary Texas Rangers sporting white Stetson hats and guns in their holsters.

After staying several days exploring the Dallas area, they woke up early one morning and drove to Guthrie, Oklahoma, near Oklahoma City to see Grandma's Aunt Mary and Uncle Ed. Aunt Mary was the sister of her mother, Martha. Her aunt and uncle had moved to Guthrie well before Oklahoma had become a state in 1907. They homesteaded 160 acres of land and lived in a dugout-type home. Grandma didn't have nearly as many relatives as Grandpa, but she loved to stay in touch with her only aunt. On the drive to Guthrie, the family stopped at the Platt National Park in south central Oklahoma. The Native Americans described this area as having magical water that would "soothe your soul and heal a sick body." Grandpa couldn't resist gulping down the magical waters. In 1976, the park was demoted to the Chickasaw National Recreation Area.

The Oklahoma City oil fields are one of the world's giant petroleum fields. Between 1900 and 1935, Oklahoma typically ranked first or second among the Mid-Continent states in oil production. However, the openings of several fields in the early 1930s coincided with the onset of the Great Depression. With the economic downturn and the glut of oil on the market, the price of crude plunged. In 1931, with the Depression at its worst, the price of oil dropped to sixteen cents a barrel, compared to $1.56 two years earlier. The Oklahoma governor ordered all wells to stop pumping until the price of oil rose back to $1.00 a barrel.

After visiting Aunt Mary in Guthrie, the family drove to Tulsa to see a burning oil well. Grandma said it was so intense that they could see, smell, and hear it for many miles. When the independent oilmen reigned in Tulsa in the 1920s, the "wildcatters" shared their wealth with the community and led efforts to build skyscrapers, an airport, and a bridge over the Arkansas River. By the 1930s, the boom was finished and many of the wildcatters fled to West Texas. However, after the Depression, the town was successful in developing many oil-related and pipeline businesses.

The local Black population felt blessed they could participate in the boom-times in Tulsa. They had created a burgeoning Greenwood district, known as the Black Wall Street, because it was a profitable and thriving community of entrepreneurs, artists, and working professionals. However, on May 31, 1921, a heavily-armed white mob, steeped in Jim Crow thinking, white supremacy, and land lust, burned and looted the town, murdering 300 people, and injuring 800 more. The governor declared martial law and sent National Guard troops to maintain order in Tulsa. Bureaucrats soon designated the altercation as a riot rather than a massacre, allowing the insurance companies to avoid paying the Black population for their losses. However, by any definition, it was a massacre. Even after a decade, my grandparents could still see the effects of the destruction.

After Tulsa, the family made an odd out-of-the-way turn east to Arkansas and Tennessee. They were on their way to Hot Springs, Arkansas, which turned out to be one of the first clues Grandpa was seeking out the trendy healing hot springs, hoping to prevent another stroke. The supposed healing powers of the hot springs go all the way back to the ancient Greeks and Romans. The hot springs come from rainwater that fell more than 4,000 years ago. It percolates 6,000 plus feet into the earth, where it becomes superheated by the surrounding rock before rising and emerging at 147 degrees Fahrenheit from the area's forty-seven hot springs.

In 1921, Congress changed the name of the Hot Springs Reservation to the Hot Springs National Park, which now encompasses 5,500 acres. The park includes the famous Bathhouse Row, which consists of eight unique, turn-of-the-century bathhouses in the heart of downtown Hot Springs. It soon became known as "The American Spa" because it attracted not only the wealthy but also health seekers from around the world. They all believed the natural thermal waters could cure any number of ailments.

It seemed like everyone was "taking the waters" as a cure for almost any malady. President Franklin D. Roosevelt made numerous visits to Warm Springs, Georgia, which he called the "Little White House." It may or may not have helped him physically, but he regained enough emotional strength to allow him to return to his great passion of politics.

The Hot Springs National Park is nestled in the picturesque woods of the Ouachita Mountains. There were dozens of hotels of varying degrees of luxury, catering to people seeking "the cure." My family chose to stay at an "autocamp" at the foot of the Hot Springs Mountain. The main feature of the camp was a large swimming pool fed by fresh running water. After this trip, Grandpa traveled a couple of times to Excelsior Springs in Missouri, hoping the waters could prevent any further strokes.

After "taking the waters," they drove fifty miles from Hot Springs to Little Rock, Arkansas, and then on to Memphis, Tennessee. When they drove through Little Rock and crossed the Arkansas River, Grandpa told the kids that this was the same wild river they crossed when they drove on the Royal Gorge bridge near Canon City, Colorado. The Arkansas River starts in the headwaters of the mountains of Colorado and meanders 1,469 miles across Colorado, Kansas, Oklahoma, and Arkansas before it spews into the Mississippi River.

Grandma wrote, "It was late when we got to Memphis and we had trouble finding a campground. When we did find one, the mosquitoes were so thick we decided to move on. It started to rain so hard we just kept right on driving and drove all night. In the morning, we were in Cape Girardeau, Missouri, where we cleaned up and had breakfast."

The last legs of the trip were the 300-mile drive on Highway 61 to Keokuk, Iowa, and another 300-mile trip to Forest City. Grandma wrote, "Iowa had never looked so good. We had no place to live so we camped at our farm until we found a house in Forest City to rent. We lived there until spring when we went back to the farm."

Gladys, the eldest daughter, who lived in Crystal Lake, wrote, "We were surprised to see them drive up and since I had not planned a meal for company, we pooled their food with ours to create the dinner for the first night home. It was so funny to see the kids spilling out of the car and running around. Everyone was very excited and we were really glad to see them. The first thing Bruce did when he got out of the car was stick his finger in the pump jack, cutting off the end of his finger. Somebody retrieved it and the doctor sewed it back on." This event served as a harbinger of family tragedies to come in the 1930s.

Keith wrote, "I was happy to be back in Iowa, but we came back to hard times, hard work, a drought, and really not much to be happy about." Pauline wrote, "In the spring of 1932, we moved back to the farm and went back to the country school. The next fall, Richard, Maxine [who married Keith after WWII] and I drove the Model A to high school in Forest City, where we boarded during the week and went home on weekends."

In the decades after this trip, the kids agreed the fifteen-month trip was life-changing and an amazing opportunity to spend time with their parents and experience over twenty national parks scattered over nineteen states. However, the rest of the 1930s was about to bring un-foreseen tragedy upon the family.

CHAPTER TEN

THE TUMULTUOUS THIRTIES

ON A CHILLY DAY IN SEPTEMBER 1932, AN EXHAUST-
ED FARMER IN WESTERN IOWA STARED OUT AT HIS
YARD AND OBSERVED EVERY PIECE OF EQUIPMENT
AND EVERY FARM ANIMAL HE OWNED, LINED UP
FOR SALE AT THE FORECLOSURE AUCTION OF HIS
PROPERTY. The bankruptcy of his farm and the fire sale of his prop-
erty represented only one of nearly a million farms in this country that
were lost to foreclosure in the early thirties. For over a decade, farmers
in this country had been locked in place with heavy mortgages, high
taxes on depressed properties, and low commodity prices.

During the go-go years of farming in the first couple of decades in
the twentieth century, the federal government encouraged farmers to
buy land, plant crops, buy new equipment to become more efficient, and

go deeply in debt. It seemed like a reasonable proposition. The thinking went that prices were so high and costs so low, that making good money seemed guaranteed. Profits went sky-high and were expected to remain that way. After all, America was feeding the world during WWI, and surely it would continue to depend upon us after the war.

But when the war was over, the government price supports were shut off, Europe quickly returned to agricultural self-sufficiency, and some farm prices plummeted nearly 50 percent. Hopeful farmers thought they would dig out of this by the end of the 1920s, but when the stock market crashed, and the Depression and Dust Bowl appeared, hope was abandoned. Farmers are a conservative bunch. They pay their bills, vote Republican, and work damn hard. However, after tolerating hundreds of forced farm auctions, and not receiving much help from anyone, the farmers across the Midwest informally organized The Farmer's Holiday Association. It was estimated that half a million Midwest farmers signed the Farmers' Holiday pledge. The idea spread like wildfire in Iowa and soon there were thirty-two local groups representing eighty-eight of the ninety-nine Iowa counties.

The Farmer's Holiday pledge had a two-phased approach. The first phase was the anti-foreclosure phase in which farmers tried to save one another from forced evictions and sales, by holding "penny sales." When a neighbor had a foreclosure auction, association members would form a pact to show up at the auction, buy the items for pennies, and then give back everything to the farmer. If the farmer could get back his equipment and animals, he could at least rent another farm and start over again.

The "penny sale" phase was working pretty well, but the next phase was more destructive, involving public blockades and strikes to prevent products from reaching the market, with the hope that a decrease in supply would raise prices. By 1932, farm prices had fallen to all-time lows of the century—corn at eight cents a bushel, pork at three cents a pound, beef at five cents a pound, oats at eleven cents a bushel, and eggs at ten cents a dozen. In many cases, the cost of raising a crop, including rent, seed, fuel, taxes, and labor, averaged about 50 percent more than the income from selling their products. Some farm families were burning their nearly worthless corn because they couldn't afford coal for their stoves. The burning corn, hovering in the air, caused the countryside to smell like popcorn.

On May 3 of 1932, a convention of 3,000 Iowa farmers called for a strike on July 4th. Their motto was, "Stay at Home-Buy Nothing-Sell Nothing." They even wrote a song for their protests:

> Let's call a Farmers' Holiday
> A Holiday let's hold
> We'll eat our wheat and ham and eggs
> And let them eat their gold.

One farmer in Woodbine said, "I'm over 60, and I've lost everything but my tongue, but I'm sure going [to go] out and use it." In late summer of 1932, hundreds of striking farmers blocked roads into Sioux City, Council Bluffs, and other towns in western Iowa, and forced farmers traveling to market, to dump their products or head back home. The angry mob dumping milk, likened themselves to the patriots who dumped tea in the Boston Harbor. But there were other protests besides dumping milk. According to the *Iowa History Journal* and other sources, about "600 farmers in LeMars, Iowa, stormed the county courthouse," grabbed a particularly punitive judge involved in farm foreclosures, put a noose around his neck, depanted him, and threatened to rob him of his manhood. A local newspaper editor arrived on the scene just in time to save the judge from hanging. There are several versions of this story, but the judge quickly left town and was never heard from again. Things got a little heated, forcing Governor Clyde Herring to call in the National Guard, and declare martial law in Plymouth County.

In July of 1932, the Dow Jones hit bottom after suffering a 90 percent loss of value from the peak in September of 1929. With the Dow Jones, farm prices, and employment hitting rock bottom, the presidential election of 1932 became a battlefield. President Hoover favored *laissez faire*, let the system correct itself theories, but the popular New York governor, Franklin D. Roosevelt, was prepared to use bold experimental remedies to revive the economy. Roosevelt won 42 of the 48 states in a landslide race, and soon appointed Iowan Henry A. Wallace as his secretary of agriculture. Together they immediately set about trying to help solve the farm crisis. On March 8, 1933, Wallace instigated the Agricultural Adjustment Act, which set limits on the size of the crops and herds farmers could produce. If a farmer agreed to limit production, he would be paid a subsidy, which helped somewhat.

After my family's delightful experience traveling through the national parks, they came home to a stark reality: disastrously low farm prices, waves of droughts, dust bowl winds, foreclosures, riots, grasshopper plagues, and sheep scams. A Montana sheep scammer sold sheep to a number of Iowa farmers, including my grandpa. He bought about two hundred sheep when they were 50 pounds, fed them to the weight of 90 pounds, and sent the sheep to the Chicago stockyards. Somehow, the Montana scammer managed to purloin all the proceeds, leaving the Iowa farmers, including my grandpa, holding the Bag Balm.

However, there must have been some hope in the air, because in February of 1933, my aunt Barbara was born and named after one of Grandma's favorite towns on the trip—Santa Barbara. Marilee remembered one time she peaked in Grandma's journal and read her words of love about Grandpa—how handsome and strong he was, how incredibly she loved him. Grandma later said that grandpa "loved to do things, just about anything that was fun. He loved to play cards and dance, and really enjoyed visiting with all the relatives on the trip."

Despite the tough economic times, an estimated 80 million people a week turned to the new talking movies, hoping to lift their spirits and rekindle their hope for the future. In 1933, Disney produced *The Three Little Pigs*, with the big bad wolf serving as a metaphor for defending oneself against the fear of what lay ahead. Mae West starred in *I'm No Angel*, and Katharine Hepburn starred in *Little Women*. The curly-topped, dimpled child star Shirley Temple appeared in her first film, *Baby Burlesks*, and the first Three Stooges comedy was released in 1934. In 1936, Charlie Chaplin released his movie, *Modern Times*, with the soulful and hopeful song: "Smile, though your heart is aching. Smile, even though its breaking. When there are clouds in the sky you'll get by. If you smile through your fear and sorrow, smile, and maybe tomorrow, you'll see the sun come shining through for you."

The 1930s was also called the Golden Age of Literary Sociology. Sinclair Lewis wrote his book, *It Can't Happen Here*, which attempted to describe how fascism might come to the US. John Steinbeck wrote *The Grapes of Wrath* and *Of Mice and Men* describing the desperation of people during the Depression. William Faulkner wrote *As I Lay Dying* and Aldous Huxley wrote *Brave New World* about a possible dystopian future for this country.

Even though there were many bread lines in the urban areas, the farm belt stayed alive eating the food they had grown themselves. For those in the cities who had the money, they could experience the excitement of the new manufactured comfort food, for this was the era that invented Spam, Kraft macaroni and cheese, Toll House chocolate chip cookies, Good Humor ice cream bars, Bisquick, Krispy Kreme doughnuts, Ritz crackers, Nestle's chocolate chips, and Kool-aid. Colonel Harland Sanders developed a secret formula of spices to flavor fried chicken, and the era of fast food emerged to haunt us for decades.

But there was more danger lurking than just the fast food. The gangster Al Capone, with his buddies, Charles "Cherry Nose" Gioe, and Louis "Cock-eyed" Fratts, had set up shop in Sioux City and Des Moines with their prostitution, gambling, and alcohol operations. But even closer to home were the activities of the gangs of bank robbers roaming the land. On March 12, 1934, John Dillinger and his gang robbed $52,000 from the First National Bank of Mason City—only 28 miles from Grandpa's farm. Dillinger entered the bank shooting his .45-caliber Thompson machine gun into the walls and ceiling, breaking the peaceful calm of the small-town Iowa city. The guard fired an 8-inch tear gas canister, but it jammed. The robbers grabbed bank employees and people on the street and forced them to serve as human shields, standing on the running boards of the speeding getaway car, a dark blue Buick sedan. This incident terrified every banker and farmer in the Midwest. By 1933, more than 9,000 banks had closed their doors and now bankers also had to worry about gangster robberies.

However, much of the tension in 1934, was caused by the waves of droughts and dust storms that hit the Great Plains. At the beginning of the century, a series of federal land acts coaxed pioneers westward by incentivizing row crop farming in the Great Plains. Previously, the land had been used mostly for cattle grazing, but new and inexperienced farmers were encouraged to plow up millions of acres of native grassland to plant wheat, corn, and other row crops. Without the deep-rooted prairie grasses to hold the topsoil, it just blew away. By 1934, it was estimated 35 million acres of land were rendered useless, and another 125 million acres were rapidly losing topsoil in the Dust Bowl states of Texas, New Mexico, Colorado, Nebraska, Kansas, and Oklahoma. To add to this tragedy, waves of droughts plagued all the farm states in 1934, 1936, and 1938. Most of these states did not have the sophisticated extension services that were available to farmers in states like Iowa. The extension services of Iowa State University had developed scientific research and extension centers giving continual advice and counsel to farmers on how to preserve the soil and other natural resources.

But the dust storms didn't just hang around the Great Plains. On the weekend of May 9-11, 1934, massive, billowing clouds of black dust two miles high blew 2,000 miles across Nebraska, Iowa, Illinois, New York City, and out to the Atlantic Ocean. Land and seas were covered with black dust that choked man and beast. One of the worst storms came on April 14, 1935, when three million tons of topsoil blew off the Great Plains, and continued the migration of up to 2.5 million people fleeing the Plains in search of a new life.

After dodging dust storms, droughts, low farm prices, and other threats, my grandparents were ready to get away, and in the late summer of 1933, they drove to Chicago to attend the Farm Bureau convention and the 1933–34 Chicago World's Fair: A Century of Progress International Exposition. According to the *Forest City Courier*, my grandpa was a delegate to the Farm Bureau Convention in Chicago in the late summer, and Grandma got to go with him to see the stunning Fair, which was situated on 424 acres on the lake shore near the Chicago museum campus. In the 1930s, the Chicago Expo was within a day's car ride for 75 percent of the population in this country. My, how this country has changed!

Over the course of two years, the *Chicago Tribune* claimed over 50 million visitors attended the Expo from all over the world. Unlike previous world fairs, this Expo raised money from the general public and corporations. "Supporters" of the fair would pay $5 and get a certificate exchangeable for ten admissions, and "Founders" of the fair paid $1000 each. This made the fair the first privately funded rather than government-funded fair, and turned out to be the only expo in history to actually make a profit.

Grandma had not had a new dress in years, but she wanted to fit in with the massive crowd of international tourists at the Expo. She studied pictures of women at the fair as well as the Sears catalog fashions of the year. Women were wearing belted, cap-sleeved white or light-colored linen or cotton dresses that fell to mid-calf. They had matching calf-length cotton coats, white gloves, and short-stocky heels. Their bobbed hair-dos were covered with a tight-fitting white cap. Grandma found some appropriate fabric and made a new dress with a matching coat that would fit in with the World's Fair crowd. She carefully packed up her new outfit and was ready for the trip.

The motto of the Expo was "Science Finds, Industry Applies, Man Adapts," touting the message that science and American life were inexplicably linked. Rather than recreating the grand Greek and Roman temples used in the 1893 Chicago Expo, the 1930 Expo used unadorned clean lines and the bold colors of contemporary and Art Deco architecture. No one wanted to hear about the glories of the past, they all craved reassurances that there would be a better tomorrow. The model homes featured a range of modern conveniences like central air conditioning and mechanical dishwashers. There was a Living Babies exhibition, showcasing premature, live babies in incubators. Thousands of spectators walked by the babies, declaring, "Hard to believe these tiny creatures would grow to become adults." General Motors set up assembly lines where 200 auto workers put together Chevrolets as 1,000 visitors at a time looked on from a viewing balcony. People could buy their car and watch it being assembled in twenty minutes.

Firestone built a tire factory where spectators could see bales of rubber transformed into auto tires. A fifteen-minute Goodyear blimp ride cost three dollars, and the Chicago Symphony Orchestra played two concerts a day. Sinclair Oil built a life-size dinosaur exhibit to remind viewers of the vast age of crude oils from which Sinclair's oil was refined. One exhibit featured cigarette-smoking robots, and another held daily shows of the scantily-clad fan dancer, Sally Rand. The first Major League Baseball All-Star Game was held at Comiskey Park in conjunction with the fair. My grandma must have been especially attracted to the Asian exhibitions, because one of her prized souvenirs was a porcelain Asian bowl, which she gifted to me decades later.

During the summer of 1933, a crowd of 125,000 people filled the nearby Soldier Field for the Jewish Day Pageant. A group of 50,000 Jews marched on Grant Park, protesting the Nazi persecution of Jews, and demanding the Expo refuse to admit Hitler's choice of Dr. Joseph Goebbels, as Germany's goodwill ambassador to the Expo. The Nazi flag was never flown at the fair.

It is such a truly American phenomena that during the worst depression and financial crisis this country had ever experienced, the wheels of innovation were still madly turning, not only for the city-folks at the Expo, but also for the farmers in the Midwest. By the mid-1930s, there were over one million gas-powered tractors in use, nearly every farmer had a car, and plans were in the works to finally electrify the rural areas. Advances were also made in creating hybrid seed corn, which allowed for better quality and yields of corn. George Washington Carver, the first African-American student at Iowa State University, received his master's in plant pathology, and researched alternative crops at the Iowa Experiment Station. In 1904, he discovered soybeans were a valuable source of protein and oil. By the 1930s, the new secretary of agriculture, Iowan Henry A. Wallace, was able to promote the increasing use of soybeans as a soil-conserving crop and a better feed for cattle. Wallace continued to experiment with breeding high-yielding strains of corn and helped create one of the largest seed corn companies in the world—Pioneer Seed Corn, and later Wallace became vice president under Roosevelt.

My grandparents were glowing when they returned back home from the exciting events of the Expo. As they settled in, they were hoping Grandpa's health was rebounding, but soon he had another stroke and their fear for the future returned. Grandpa was strong and bounded back from this stroke, but decided he needed once again to "take the waters" and revive his health at Excelsior Springs in Missouri.

In August of 1934, my grandparents loaded eighteen-month-old Barbara and five-year-old Marilee in their trusty Model A Ford, and drove 300 miles straight south to "America's Haven of Health." They stayed in a room in the Boarding House District and Grandpa submerged himself in the healing waters of the springs. Even during the Depression and the worst farm crisis in history, attendance at the springs was robust, and the family quickly got into the routine.

Marilee remembered one morning in particular. Grandpa got up early, made oatmeal for everyone, and they all walked him to the springs so he could soak in the mineral baths. Meanwhile, back in Iowa, the *Forest City Courier* later reported that my uncle Donald, was enroute to buy livestock and pulled into a filling station in Osceola, forty miles south of Des Moines. The station attendant noticed Donald's Hancock County license plate and asked him if he was from Crystal Lake. When the attendant learned Donald was a Cottington, he told him that he had just heard a Des Moines WHO radio broadcast strongly advising

Levi Cottington come home quickly, as there had been a bad accident. Donald drove to the nearest telegram office and quickly sent a message to Grandpa: Come home to the Buffalo Center hospital now!

Grandma heard a knock on the door of her room in Excelsior Springs, and was handed a telegram. She packed up the kids and ran off to get Grandpa. Grandpa made a quick decision—he could make the 300-mile trip back much faster if he put Grandma and the kids on a bus, allowing him to test the mettle of the Model A Ford and rush 65 mph pell-mell back to Forest City. When he arrived at the hospital, the family told him what had happened. The *Forest City Courier* later reported, "The accident occurred at the Carl Bergdahl place, where [Grandpa's third son] Dwight and others were threshing. Dwight had gone into the field with others to spread shocks [stacking cut grain in upright bundles], and when the work had been finished, he returned to the wagon to get his shotgun to do some hunting. When he reached for the gun, the trigger caught on a nail, and the weapon discharged, striking him in the stomach." Dwight was rushed to the Buffalo Center hospital, but died shortly after arriving. Grandpa collapsed in grief. This was an accident from which he would never recover.

Dwight was only twenty-one years old, with a wife, Ruth, and a baby, Nina Mae. Ruth was pregnant at the time and about five months after the accident, gave birth to Dwight Jr. in January of 1935. Dwight was tall, dark, rugged, very kind, and very handsome. The family missed him tremendously.

The family recalled that after the death of Dwight, Grandpa was so devastated that he was never the same. They struggled through the fall and tried to prepare for a hopeful Christmas, but it was not to be. Just before the holidays, in the snow-covered ground, Grandpa had a final massive stroke, which left him in a catatonic and vegetated state, lasting for almost two years. He could not move or respond to anyone or anything. Grandma and the kids put him in a bed in the living room near the vent from the coal furnace, so he would be warm during the long winter.

Grandma sat down in the dark living room watching Grandpa, and faced the reality that her life was going to become much more challenging. Grandpa could not work anymore, he couldn't talk, he couldn't move, the bright light was gone from his eyes, and he was unresponsive to touch and sound. He had to be fed, bathed, and shaved. Grandma was thirty-nine years old and was now responsible for a 360-acre farm, eleven children, and a catatonic husband, in the middle of the Depression, a severe farm crisis, record cold winters, and a dust storm. She looked at Grandpa lying there in a vegetated state, gently touched his check, and told him she was pregnant again, and if it was a boy, he would be named Levi.

Marilee remembered Grandma showed unbelievable strength and endurance during that time. Grandma never complained, never raised her voice, never felt sorry for herself. She presented this strength and her indefatigable nature to her children, so they too could get through those trying times. Grandma never drank or took the Lord's name in vain. However, she was known to mutter Pshaw!, when she was struck with disbelief about something and was known to utter *bescheuert* when she thought someone was one cupcake short of a picnic. My uncle Keith said she was of strong, bull-headed German stock, and although many farmers in the area were not able to keep up the mortgage payments, she always managed to raise the money to pay the $1,200 annual mortgage and the $300 property tax.

Every one of the kids had jobs to do. Of the two eldest sons at home, Keith was seventeen and my dad, Richard, was fourteen, so they both assumed the duties of planting the crops in the spring, and taking care of the larger animals. Of the eldest daughters at home, Pauline was sixteen, and Gwen was twelve. Marilee said her duties were "collecting corn cobs from the pigs and trimming the wicks in the kerosene lamps. Pauline didn't like to cook so she did the sewing and cleaning and Gwen helped with the cooking." They all took care of some of the housework, laundry, gardening, and care for the smaller children and animals. The smaller children pitched in when they could.

Grandma's Papa Herman, true to form, refused to help her. She probably wouldn't have taken his money anyway. Grandma later told me that her friends and neighbors urged her to go on welfare, but she refused. She was a proud, hard-working woman, and she was going to be brave and strong and help her children endure these endless waves of heartbreak.

Times were tough for the family, but everyone was having a tough time. The basic forms of entertainment for most families were movies, board games, sports, and the radio. Every night the family would gather around the battery-powered radio and listen to their favorite shows—*Abbott & Costello*, *The Adventures of Ozzie and Harriet*, *Amos & Andy*, *Dick Tracy*, and *Fibber McGee and Molly*. One of Marilee's favorite shows was *The Answer Man*, hosted by Albert Carlyle Mitchell, who with a staff of forty, was situated across from the New York Public Library. They received over 2,500 questions a day, some of which would be answered on the air: How many buffalo would it take to fill the Grand Canyon? Do birds dream? The show was a precursor to the modern-day google. One day Marilee looked outside and saw tiny frogs falling down with the rain. She ran into the kitchen and exclaimed—It's raining frogs! No one believed her, so she wrote to The Answer Man with her question—can it rain frogs? The answer came back—Yes! Frog rain is a rare meteorological phenomenon in which frogs get swept up in a storm, travel miles, and then fall from the sky when the clouds release the water. Marilee proudly felt vindicated, which is a great feeling for an eight-year-old.

The family had to cut costs everywhere. They had to go back to using the kerosene lamps, because they could no longer afford batteries for the electric lighting system their dad had built. Grandma collected used clothing from relatives and friends, and with her superior sewing skills, made lovely dresses and coats for the older girls. They had to lay off their farm hands and assume the jobs themselves. At one point, Keith sold one of the cows to buy his mother a time-saving Maytag gas-powered washing machine. Yet, at no time did they feel poor or destitute. They had enough food on the farm, they had their family and friends, and everyone seemed to be in the same boat.

During the summer of 1935, Grandma was having pregnancy problems with swollen legs and other issues and her doctor advised that she have her baby at a hospital. After bearing eight children at home with Grandpa's help, Grandma had her ninth child, Levi III, in a hospital, on July 31, 1935. During one of the hottest, most humid summers, Grandma placed the baby near his father, hoping they both could somehow grab a cool breeze from the open windows in the living room.

But times were getting even tougher, as the winters of 1934 and 1936 produced massive snow storms that kept the family isolated for days at the farm house. The summer of 1936 was considered the worst, hottest, driest summer in Iowa history. It became difficult to keep Grandpa warm in the winter and cool in the summer. They had to take him out to the porch during the hot summer nights, to try to cool him off.

All over the state, crops dried up and the livestock died for lack of food. Along with the hot and dry conditions came enormous numbers of grasshoppers and chinch bugs, who ate some of the remaining crops in the state. Crop insurance wasn't available until 1938, so some farmers lost everything. Almost 5,000 people nationwide perished during the drought, roughly 400 were from Iowa. The severity of the drought forever changed the landscape and history of Iowa, and prompted the use of irrigation, tiered fields, and other water-saving techniques.

During the night of April 5th, 1937, Grandpa passed away. Marilee recalled, "When we came downstairs in the morning, mother told us he had died and I walked over to his bed and touched him to see if he was really dead. His body was taken to the funeral home in Forest City, brought back to the farm for the funeral, and then taken to the Graceland Cemetery in Webster City to be buried next to his parents and his son, Dwight."

The article in the *Forest City Courier* read:

> We mourn the passing of a devoted husband and father. His nine children at home and the older ones have carried on bravely during the years of their

father's illness. He was an unusually affectionate and thoughtful man to his family and his memory will be cherished by his children as his influence will long be felt in their lives. He was always a good neighbor, a loyal friend, and a good citizen. He was the Secretary of the Winnebago County Fair, and held various offices in the local and county Farm Bureau. The high esteem in which he was held by all who knew him, was shown by the many neighborly kindnesses offered during his prolonged illness.

My grandparents' dearest friend, Dr. Effie McCollum Jones, pastor of the Universalist Church in Webster City, conducted both services. Grandpa's two favorite songs were sung at the church: Crossing the Bar and The Old Rugged Cross.

> And I'll cherish the old rugged cross
> Till my trophies at last I lay down
> And I will cling to the old rugged cross
> And exchange it some day for a crown

THE WINDS OF WAR

AT THE END OF THE 1930S, THE FARM ECONOMY WAS STARTING TO GET BETTER, BUT THE WINDS OF WAR WERE BLOWING HARD THROUGH EUROPE AND ASIA. Earlier in the decade, the Nazis had burned the German Reichstag and destroyed the German democracy. Their new chancellor, Adolf Hitler, was on his way to supreme dictatorship and he was already planning the expansion of his kingdom. On the Asian front, Japan invaded Manchuria and declared war on China, a country that didn't put up a strong resistance.

In March of 1938, German troops invaded Austria and annexed them into the Reich. Later in the year, the Munich Pact, signed by the French Premier Daladier, the British Prime Minister Chamberlain, Hitler, and Italy's Mussolini, allowed Germany to annex western Czechoslovakia. Their hope was that the annexation would prevent a war or invasions of more countries. Winston Churchill was apoplectic and disagreed with their decision, declaring, "You were given the choice of war or dishonor and you chose dishonor and you will have war!" Churchill was right. Hitler was not content with just parts of Czechoslovakia, he wanted it all. In 1939, Hitler's troops seized the rest of the Czech country and invaded Poland, violating the Munich Pact. In 1940, German soldiers stormed through Denmark, Belgium, the Netherlands, Luxembourg, and France. Hitler also implemented "Operation Sea Lion," an intense eight-month bombing campaign of England.

Meanwhile, Grandma was watching the winds of war with trepidation. She knew if it escalated, America would join the war and she had five sons who would be eligible for the draft. After a couple of years of trying to run the 360-acre farm as a widow with nine children at home, she decided to downsize. In late 1939, Grandma sold the farm and found a much smaller farm in Bode, Iowa, about sixty miles southwest of Forest City. When Grandpa died in April of 1937, my father, Richard, had to quit high school in order to help Keith and Grandma run the farm, but all three of them were starting to get exhausted with farming.

In early 1941, Keith joined the army and Lyle joined the Marine Corps. Things escalated when, on December 7, the Japanese bombed Pearl Harbor and the American-held Philippines, Guam, and Wake Island, as well as the British-held Malaya, Singapore, and Hong Kong. A day later President Roosevelt and Congress declared war on Japan. This prompted Germany to declare war on the United States, which led to the US declaring war on Germany on December 11.

There was a total of 16 million Americans who served in World War II, and Grandma committed six of her children to that effort. In 1942, Rex joined the Army Air Corp in the South Pacific, flying B-24 bombers; my father, Richard, joined the navy in the South Pacific, and Pauline joined the Navy Waves.

In November of 1942, there was a radio announcement that a ship in the Pacific had been attacked by Japan and sunk. Hundreds of sailors were killed. Grandma listened intently and glanced at her Blue Star Flag in the window, which announced she had four sons and one daughter valiantly serving in the war. She went through her mental trapline. Keith was in the army in Africa, Lyle was in the Marine Corp, but both Rex and Richard were on ships in the South Pacific. There were continuing rumors that Iowans were on the ship that sank. Grandma held her breath and prayed for the safety of her sons. This was about the time that fifteen-year-old Bruce started pestering his mom to certify him as seventeen, so he could go fight with his brothers. Grandma demurred. That's all she needed—six of her children serving in the war at the same time. Several months later she finally capitulated and signed the letter so Bruce could go to war at the tender age of sixteen.

Finally, the news came in. The USS *Juneau* sank in November 1942, in the naval battle of Guadalcanal in the Solomon Sea. The ship had been hit by the Japanese, there was a great explosion, the *Juneau* broke in two, and disappeared in just twenty seconds. A total of 687 men were instantly killed, but about 100 sailors survived the sinking and were left to fend for themselves in the shark-infested waters for eight days before they were rescued. There were Iowans killed, but the news was slow in coming. Grandma kept one eye on her Blue Star Flag and the other eye on the driveway. She knew that a uniformed man coming up her driveway would portend heartache.

The heartache did come, but not yet to Bode. The Sullivan family in Waterloo, Iowa, lost all five of their sons in the sinking of the USS *Juneau*. It was the greatest combat-related loss by a single family in this country. Grandma sat down to write a letter to the mother of the Sullivan children. They had much in common. They both had five sons serving in the war. Grandma understood the unjust nature of the war and the capricious and devastating impact of the death of loved ones. She was still keenly feeling the loss of her husband and her son, Dwight, so she was sensitive to the injustice of it all. A neighbor in Bode who had just lost her only son in the war, angrily told Grandma, "You have five sons serving in the war, and I only had one. It should have been one of your sons who was killed." What can you possibly say to a mother who has experienced such a tragedy?

Year after year, the war dragged on. One day grandma saw a uniformed man coming up the driveway. She glanced at her blue star flag and slowly opened the front door. The news was grim. Keith was seriously wounded in a battle in Africa and was taken to a hospital. She waited and prayed and weeks later the men of gloom once again marched up her driveway. Keith was doing much better, but Richard was taken to a hospital in California with a serious case of rheumatic fever. My mother, who had just married my dad, Richard, immediately grabbed her new sister-in-law, Gwen, and they got on a train and headed to California to be with Richard.

So now there were only three children left at home: Levi III, Marilee, and Barbara and Grandma knew they couldn't continue to run the farm. In February of 1944, Grandma sold her Bode farm at auction for $200 an acre. This was a pretty good price, because land in the area was selling for an average of $158 an acre. There are five major areas of farmland in Iowa: Western livestock, central grain, northeast dairy, eastern livestock, and southern pastures. The central grain area where Grandma lived, typically had the highest land values. In May of 1944, after Levi III finished school, Grandma grabbed the younger kids and moved to Des Moines. She settled in a home near Drake University. According to an article in the *Des Moines Register*, Grandma found a job as a hostess in a church near Drake. It was a new type of position for the church to put someone in charge of arranging and catering all the events: weddings, funerals, holiday festivities. Grandma put her business degree and her extensive management skills learned from farming and built a successful career at the church, while she waited for her sons to return from the war.

On May 8, 1945, the German armed forces surrendered unconditionally and Victory in Europe Day (V-E Day) was proclaimed. Four months later, the official Victory over Japan Day (V-J Day) was declared when the formal surrender documents were signed aboard the USS *Missouri*.

Lyle served in the Marine Corps.

Keith served in the 34th Red Bull Division
of the Army until August of 1945 after
the campaigns in Africa, Italy, and
Germany won him many medals including
the Purple Heart.

Pauline served as a nurse in the Navy Waves.

Richard was on a navy destroyer headed
for battles in Japan when he heard of the
Japanese surrender.

Rex flew B-24 bombers for the Army
Air Corps in the South Pacific.

Bruce, enlisting at the tender age
of sixteen, was in the 4th Marine
Division in the Pacific Theatre and
fought in seven battles. He made three
landings in the Philippines and was
involved in the last battle at Okinawa
on Easter Island. He also fought in
the Korean War.

Bus Rolland (Gwen's husband)
served in the army.

Dr. Jim Watson (Pauline's
husband) served in the navy as a
Pharmacists Mate and cared for
the wounded on D-Day.

A few years later Levi III served
in the Navy Honor Guard.

Bode Honor Roll

All of Grandma's children and sons-in-law came home safely to her.

The town of Bode during WWII had a population of only 500, but more than 114 men in town served in the war.

At the beginning of this book, I mentioned how impactful my grandparents had been in my life. Even though I never met my grandpa, the more I discovered about him, the closer I felt to his spirit. The values of past generations of my family can be seen in the current generations. The frugality they learned during the Depression lives on in my generation. The ability of Grandma to persevere in impossible conditions during the 1930s, has been instructional for all of us as we face the crises in our lives. The pride our parents had in their military service has stayed with us as many of my cousins unselfishly served their country. Our grandparents love of adventure, curiosity and travel inspired us all to learn more about our world. My grandma's sense of justice, equality, ethics, and fairness to everyone guides us in our daily decisions, as many of us have volunteered to make our communities a better place to live. Our grandparents' hard work and independence are evident in the accomplishments of their thirty-six grandchildren: a professional basketball player, a university head basketball coach, a US Navy jet pilot, an emergency room medical professional, vice chair of a multi-billion-dollar bank, and an award-winning author. And those are just the girls.

Despite all the tragedies the family experienced in the 1930s and 1940s, with Grandma's love and guidance, we all grew and prospered.

1964 Cottington Family Reunion

NATIONAL PARKS, NATIONAL FORESTS, AND CITIES VISITED ON THE TRIP.

NINETEEN STATES, THREE COUNTRIES, TWENTY-FIVE NATIONAL PARKS, IN FIFTEEN MONTHS. *(Some areas became National Parks after the trip. Each national park has the year it became a park in parentheses.)*

IOWA
+ Webster City, Crystal Lake, Ayrshire

SOUTH DAKOTA
+ Mitchell, Wall, Rapid City
+ Mount Rushmore National Memorial

- Harney Peak (Now called Black Elk Peak)
- Grand River National Grassland
- Wind Cave National Park (1903)
- Badlands National Park (1978)
- Black Hills National Forest

NORTH DAKOTA

- Turtle Lake, Bismarck
- Little Missouri National Grassland
- Sullys Hill National Park (1904, turned into wildlife preserve in 1931)
- Theodore Roosevelt National Park (1978)

MONTANA

- Billings, Bozeman, Butte, Missoula, Deer Lodge Pass
- Bitterroot National Forest

WYOMING

- Yellowstone National Park (1872)
- Grand Teton National Park (1929)
- Shoshone National Forest

IDAHO

- Coeur d'Alene

WASHINGTON and trip to CANADA

- Spokane, Wenatchee, Bellingham, Seattle, Puyallup
- North Cascades National Park (1968)
- Olympic National Park (1938) viewed from Seattle
- Rainier National Park (1899)
- Okanogan-Wenatchee National Forest
- Mount Baker-Snoqualmie National Forest
- Gifford Pinchot National Forest

OREGON
+ Portland, Eugene, Harrisburg
+ Willamette National Forest

CALIFORNIA and trip to Mexico
+ Crescent City, Eureka, San Francisco
+ Redwood National Park (1968)
+ Los Angeles, Compton, Santa Barbara, San Diego, Hemet
+ Yosemite National Park (1890)
+ Sequoia National Park (1890)
+ Kings Canyon National Park (1940)
+ General Grant National Park (1890) consumed into Kings Canyon in 1940
+ Joshua Tree National Park (1994)
+ Mojave Desert, Needles

NEVADA
+ Boulder Dam (Now called Hoover Dam)

ARIZONA
+ Phoenix, Flagstaff
+ Grand Canyon National Park (1919)
+ Painted Desert and Petrified Forest National Park (1962)

UTAH
+ Salt Lake City
+ Zion National Park (1919) National Monument 1909
+ Bryce National Park (1928) National Monument 1923

COLORADO
+ Grand Junction, Montrose, Gunnison, Denver, Colorado Springs
+ Black Canyon of Gunnison National Park (1999) National Monument 1933

- Wind Cave National Park (1903)
- Great Sand Dunes National Park (2004) National Monument 1932
- Monarch Pass
- Royal Gorge Bridge and Park
- Rocky Mountains National Park (1915)
- Estes Park

NEW MEXICO

- Santa Fe, Taos
- Puye Cliff Dwellings

TEXAS

- Wichita Falls, Fort Worth, Dallas

OKLAHOMA

- Guthrie, Oklahoma City, Tulsa
- Platt National Park (1902) (In 1976 was changed to Chickasaw National Recreation Area)

ARKANSAS

- Fort Smith, Little Rock, Hot Springs
- Hot Springs National Park (1921)

TENNESSEE

- Memphis

MISSOURI

- Cape Girardeau

PUBLICATIONS THAT HELPED US WITH RESEARCH

Chapter One: 1929: Levi's Dream

- 1928 Sears Roebuck Catalog
- *An Ordinary Adventure, Retracing Mom and Grandpa's 1934 Trip on Route 66,* Diane Wood, 2018
- *By Motor to the Golden Gate,* Emily Post, 1916
- *Vail, Duster, and Tire Iron,* Alice Ramsey, 2005, republished
- *A Reliable Car and a Woman Who Knows It,* Curt McConnell, 2000
- *Down the Asphalt Path: The Automobile and the American City,* Clay McShane, 1995
- *Eat My Dust: Early Woman Motorists,* Georgine Clarsen, 2008
- *Sunset Magazine,* "Alone Across the Continent: The Adventures of a Woman Motorist on the Road from Coast to Coast," Maud Younger, 1924
- *Dressed for Freedom: The Fashionable Politics of American Feminism,* Einav Rabinovitch-Fox, 2021
- *Women's Home Companion,* "Following the Open Road in Your Car," 1925

- *Literary Digest*, "A Woman's Advice on Motor Camping," 1925
- *Setting a Course: American Women in the 1920s*, Dorothy Brown, 1987
- *Taking the Wheel: Women and the Coming of the Motor Age*, Virginia Scharff, 1991
- *The Complete Official Road Guide of the Lincoln Highway*, Lincoln Highway Association, 1915
- *The Lincoln Highway: The Crusade that Made Transportation History*, Lincoln Highway Association, reprinted in 2018
- *The Lincoln Highway: A Road Trip Celebration of America's First Coast-to-Coast Highway*, Brian Butko, 2019
- *The Road Guide of the Lincoln Highway*, 1916
- *The Lincoln Highway: The Great American Road Trip*, Michael Wallis, 2007
- *American Road: The Story of an Epic Transcontinental Journal at the Dawn of the Motor Age*, Pete Davies, 2002
- *Driving While Black*, Gretchen Sorin, 2020
- *Hotel: An American History*, Andrew Sandoval-Strausz, 2007
- *Going West in a Model T Ford*, James Burdick, Jim Kackeison, 2017
- *Nothing Like it in the World: The Men Who Built the Transcontinental Railroad 1863–1869*, Stephen Ambrose, 2001
- *The Oregon Trail: A New American Journey*, Rinker Buck, 2016
- *The Father of Route 66*, Susan Croce Kelly, reprint 2019

Chapter Two: 1909–1920: The Golden Age of Agriculture

- *Pandemic 1918: Eyewitness Accounts from the Greatest Medical Holocaust in Modern History*, Catherine Arnold, 2020
- *The Great Influenza: The Story of the Deadliest Pandemic in History*, John M. Barry, 2005
- *Pale Rider: The Spanish Flu of 1918 and How It Changed the World*, Laura Spinney, 2017
- *The 1918 Spanish Influenza Pandemic*, David Anversa, 2020
- *The Influenza Pandemic of 1918–1919: A Brief History with Documents*, Susan Kingley Kent, 2012
- *Influenza Encyclopedia: The American Influenza Epidemic of 1918–1919*
- *The Des Moines Register*, articles during the Influenza
- *America's Forgotten Pandemic: The Influenza of 1918*, 2nd edition, Alfred W. Crosby

- *The Vagabonds: The Story of Henry Ford and Thomas Edison's Ten-Year Road Trip*, Jeff Guinn, 2019
- *Uncommon Friends: Life with Thomas Edison, Henry Ford, Harvey Firestone, Alexis Carrel, and Charles Lindberg*, James Newton, 1989
- *Men and Rubber: The Story of Business*, Harvey Firestone, 1926
- *Down the Asphalt Path: The Automobile and the American City*, Clay McShane, 1994
- *Americans on the Road: From Autocamp to Motel, 1910–1945*, Warren James Belasco, 1979
- *The People's Tycoon: Henry Ford and the American Century*, Steven Watts, 2006
- *My Life and Work: Autobiography of Henry Ford*, Henry Ford and Samuel Crowther, 1922
- *Today and Tomorrow*, Henry Ford, 1926
- *Moving Forward*, Henry Ford, 1930
- *The Public Image of Henry Ford: An American Folk Hero and His Company*, David L. Lewis, 1987

Chapter Three: The 1920s on an Iowa Farm

- *Iowa: The Middle Land*, Dorothy Schwieder, 1996
- *Grandmother Brown's Hundred Years 1827–1927: Settling the Midwest*, Harriet Connor Brown, 2016
- *Days on the Family Farm: From the Golden Age through the Great Depression*, Carrie A. Meyer, 2007
- *Little Heathens: Hard Times and High Spirits on an Iowa Farm During the Great Depression*, Mildred Armstrong Kalish, 2008
- *Anxious Decades: America in Prosperity and Depression: 1920–1941*, Michael Parrish, 1994
- *1929: Book One*, M.L. Gardner, 2011
- *Trends in Farm Land Values in the US from 1912 to 1928*, Karl Scholz, 1929
- *NBER, American Agriculture, 1899–1939: A Study of Output, Employment, and Productivity*, Harold Barger and Hans Landsberg, 1942
- *Wheat: Ratio of Exports to Net Output, 1897 to 1938*
- *Whereby We Thrive: A History of American Farming*, John Schlebecker, 1975
- *Open Country Iowa: Rural Women, Tradition and Change*, Deborah Fink, 1986
- *Women and Farming: Changing Roles, Changing Structures*, Haney and Knowles, 1988

- Kendall Young Library, Webster City, Iowa
- 1904 Business Directory of Webster City
- *Iowa Heritage Illustrated*, various articles
- *A Good Day's Work: An Iowa Farm in the Great Depression*, Dwight Hoover, 2007
- *The Concise History of Woman Suffrage*, Mari Jo Buhle and Paul Buhle, 2005
- *Only Yesterday: An Informal History of the 1920s*, Frederick Lewis Allen, 2011
- *Report of the Country Life Commission*, Theodore Roosevelt, 1909
- *Farmer's Almanac: Traditional Home Remedies: Time-Tested Methods for Staying Well-the Natural Way*, Martha White, 1997
- *The Best of the Old Farmer's Almanac*, Judson Hale, 1992
- *The Webster City Freeman-Tribune*, various articles in the 1910s through 1940s
- *The Webster City Daily Freeman*, various articles in the 1910s through 1940s

Chapter Four: 1926: You're Ahead in a Ford All the Way. From the Model T to the Model A

- *The Ford Model A: A Collectors Originality Guide*, Jim Schild, 2009
- *The Essential Buyer's Guide Ford Model A 1927–1931*, John Buckley and Mike Codell, 2018
- *The Legendary Model A Ford: The Ultimate History of One of America's Great Automobiles*, Peter Winnewisser, 1999
- *Iowa's Automobiles, an Entertaining and Enlightening History*, Bill Jepsen, 2007
- *The Ford Model A*, Robert Kreipke, 2020
- *The Beginners Guide to the Model A Ford 1928–1931*, Les Pearson, 2013
- *The Ford Model A Car: Construction—Operation—Repair*, Victor Page, 1929
- *Model A Ford Troubleshooting and Diagnostics*, Les Andrews, 2000
- *The Magazine of Business*, "Nomadic America's $3,300,000,000 Market," July, 1927
- *Henry's Lady: An Illustrated History of the Model A Ford*, Ray Miller, 1972
- *The Automobile Age*, James J. Flink, 1990
- *My Years with General Motors*, Alfred P. Sloan Jr., 1990

Chapter Five: The Trip Begins: Crystal Lake to Cody, Wyoming
- *Buffalo Bill's Town in the Rockies*, Jeannie Cook, 1996

- *The Power of Scenery: Frederick Law Olmsted and the Origin of the National Parks*, Dennis Drabelle, 2021
- *The Lakotas and the Black Hills: The Struggle for Sacred Ground*, Jeffrey Ostler, 2011
- *Buffalo Bill's America: William Cody and the Wild West Show*, Louis S. Warren, 2006

Chapter Six: Yellowstone National Park in 1930

- *Yellowstone: A Wilderness Besieged*, Richard A. Bartlett, 1985
- *The Stories of Yellowstone: Adventure Tales from the World's First National Park*, M. Mark Miller, 2014
- *The Great Divide: Travels in the Upper Yellowstone in the Summer of 1874 and Hunting in Yellowstone*, Windham-Quin Earl of Dunraven, reprinted in 2018
- *Yellowstone Library and Museum Association*, Yellowstone Research Library
- *Dude Ranching in Yellowstone Country*, W. Hudson Kensel, 2022
- *Your Guide to the National Parks: The Complete Guide to All 63 National Parks*, Michael Joseph Oswald, 2022
- *In Search of the Golden West: The Tourist in Western America*, Earl Pomeroy, 1957
- *Empire of Shadows: The Epic Story of Yellowstone*, George Black, 2012
- *The Devil Wagon in God's Country: The Automobile and Social Change in Rural America, 1893-1929*, Michael Berger, 1979

Chapter Seven: On the Way to the West Coast

- *A History of Wenatchee: The Apple Capital of the World*, John A. Gellatly, 1962
- *Wenatchee, Images of America*, Wenatchee Valley Museum and Cultural Center, 2012
- *History of Reedsburg and the Upper Baraboo Valley, State of Wisconsin*, Merton Edwin Krug, 1929
- *The Oregon Trail: A New American Journey*, Rinker Buck, 2016
- *Railroaded: The Transcontinentals Making of Modern America*, Richard White, 2012
- *Crazy Horse and Custer: The Parallel Lives of Two American Warriors*, Stephen E. Ambrose, 1996
- *History of Reedsburg*, Forgotten Books, 2017

- *Seattle: A Fresh Look at One of America's Most Exciting Cities*, Nard Jones, 1972
- *Skid Row: An Informal Portrait of Seattle*, Murray Morgan, 2018
- *In the City of Neighborhoods: Seattle's History of Community Activism*, Arthur J. O'Donnell, 2004
- *Olmsted in Seattle: Creating a Park System for a Modern City*, Jennifer Ott, 2019
- *The Seattle General Strike*, Robert L. Friedheim, 2018
- *King County and Its Emerald City: Seattle, An Illustrated History*, James R. Warren, 1997
- *San Francisco Earthquake: A Minute-by-Minute Account of the 1906 Disaster*, Gordon Thomas, 2014

Chapter Eight: Living the Life in Compton, California 1930–31

- *LA Noir: The Struggle for the Soul of America's Most Seductive City*, John Buntin, 2010
- *WPA Guide to California, WPA Guide to LA*, Federal Writers' Project, 1939
- *Oil!*, Upton Sinclair, 1933
- *The Winning of the West*, Theodore Roosevelt, 1888
- *A Century of Dishonor: The Classic Exposé of the Plight of the Native Americans*, Helen Hunt Jackson, 1885
- *Decade of Betrayal: Mexican Repatriation in the 1930s*, Francisco E. Balderrama, 2006
- *California: A History*, Kevin Starr, 2005
- *The San Francisco Earthquake: A Minute-by-Minute Account of the 1906 Disaster*, Gordon Thomas, Max Morgan-Witts, 2014
- *Joshua Tree National Park: A History of Preservation of the Desert*, Larry M. Dilsaver, 2015

Chapter Nine: Home to Iowa 1931

- *Appetite for America: How Visionary Businessman Fred Harvey Built a Railroad Hospitality Empire That Civilized the Wild West*, Stephen Fried, 2010
- *Tulsa Race Massacre of 1921: The History of Black Wall Street, and its Destruction in America's Worst and Most Controversial Racial Riot*, Independently published, 2020
- *Tulsa's Black Wall Street: The Story of Greenwood*, David L. Payne, 2018

Chapter Ten: The Tumultuous Thirties

- *Since Yesterday: The 1930s in America*, Frederick L. Allen, 1986
- *The WPA Guide to Iowa*, Federal Writers' Project of the WPA, 1939
- *A Century of Progress: A Photographic Tour of the 1933–34 Chicago World's Fair*, Chicago Tribune Staff, 2015
- *Chicago 1933 World's Fair: A Century of Progress in Photographs*, Mark Bussler, 2019
- *The 1933 Chicago World's Fair: A Century of Progress*, Cheryl R. Ganz, 2012
- *Statistical History of the US*, Fairfield Publishers, 1965
- *The Age of the Great Depression*, Dixon Wector, 1971
- *The Bumpy Road: Farm Life in the Great Depression*, Quentin F. Veit, 1985
- *Corn and It's Early Fathers*, Henry A. Wallace, 1956
- *Duty and Debt to the Farmer*, Henry C. Wallace, 1925
- *The Hybrid Corn Makers: Prophets of Plenty*, A. Richard Crabb, 2011
- *The Grapes of Wrath*, John Steinbeck, 1939
- *The Great Crash 1929*, John Kenneth Galbraith, 2009
- *Lords of Finance: The Bankers Who Broke the World*, Liaquat Ahamed, 2009
- *Hard Times: An Oral History of the Great Depression*, Studs Terkel, 2011
- *The Coming of the New Deal: 1933–1935: The Age of Roosevelt*, Arthur M. Schlesinger Jr., 2003
- *Once in Golconda: A True Drama of Wall Street, 1920-1938*, John Brooks, 2014
- *The Day the Bubble Burst: A Social History of the Wall Street Crash of 1929*, Gordon Thomas and Max Morgan-Witts, 2014
- *1939: A People's History of the Coming of the Second World War*, Frederick Taylor, 2021
- *Nothing is Too Big to Fail: How the Last Financial Crisis Informs Today*, Linda and Kerry Killinger, 2021
- *The Worst Hard Time: The Untold Story of Those who Survived the Great American Dust Bowl*, Timothy Egan, 2006
- *Agricultural Discontent in the Middle West, 1900–1939*, Saloutos and Hicks, 2008
- *Struggle for Land Ownership in Iowa*, article by W. G. Murray, Iowa State
- *The Mantz Trilogy: Three Miles Square, The Road Returns and County Seat*, Paul Corey, 1939
- *1929: The Year of the Great Crash*, Klingaman, 1989

- Rural Electrification Act of 1935, The Agriculture Adjustment Act of 1938
- *It Can't Happen Here*, Sinclair Lewis, 1935
- *The Grapes of Wrath* and *Of Mice and Men*, John Steinbeck, 1939 and 1937
- *As I Lay Dying*, William Faulkner, 1991
- *Look Homeward Angel*, Thomas Wolfe, 1929
- *Brave New World*, Aldous Huxley, 1932
- *Consumers in the Country: Technology and Social Change in Rural America*, Ronald Kline, US Census Bureau, 2000
- *Whereby We Thrive: A History of American Farming*, John Schlebecker, Iowa State, 1975

ABOUT THE AUTHORS

Kerry Killinger and Linda Cottington Killinger are the authors of the prize-winning and best-selling book, *Nothing is Too Big to Fail: How the Last Financial Crisis Informs Today*. They have won the Nautilus Award for Journalism and Investigative Reporting, Axiom Business Award for Economics, IPPY Award for Finance and Economics, and the Indie Award for Business. Both have had long careers in finance and banking.

Marilee Cottington McAlpine is Linda's 94-year-old aunt, who was a one-year-old on the 1930 trip. She has a degree in business education from the University of Minnesota and taught business and English in a number of states as well as other countries around the world. All three authors live in the Seattle area and for decades have shared the love of boating and travel.

All proceeds from the sale of this book will be donated to charity via The Kerry and Linda Killinger Foundation. Visit our website, thekillingerfoundation.org.

ACKNOWLEDGMENTS

We are very appreciative of our publisher, David Wilk, of Prospecta Press, who graciously gave us great ideas, encouragement, and support during the entire process. Thanks to our copy editor, Jeremy Townsend, who is a master at grammar, and helped us with ideas and support.

We received a tremendous amount of support from Scott Cottington, who is the keeper of the family flame and the documents. Special thanks go to Tricia Wood and Lori Cliff for their help in sending family postcards and other pictures, and also to Jill Morelli, for sharing her genealogy expertise.

Special appreciation goes to Linda's grandma, who persevered graciously through all the crises in her life, while providing inspiration to all of her thirty-six grandchildren.